SPRING BOOKS LONDON

Birds of Field and Forest

BIRDS

of Field and Forest

Illustrations by
E. DEMARTINI

Introduction by
O. ŠTĚPÁNEK

SPRING BOOKS

Designed and produced by ARTIA for
SPRING BOOKS
Spring House · Spring Place · London N W 5
S 800

BIRDS are probably the most popular of all the members of the animal kingdom. People like to hear the song of the lark and the nightingale, to watch the flight of the eagle and the falcon; they find pleasure in hearing the voice of the cuckoo in the woods or of quail in the fields, the twitter of swallows and the cooing of pigeons. That is no doubt the reason why birds are so often to be found in fairy tales and folk songs. And it is not only the legendary Phoenix but the common sparrow, the cuckoo, the lark, the nightingale, the crow and the raven which figure in these stories and in numerous fables and proverbs.

It is therefore somewhat ironic that it should be birds which suffer most as a result of human interference with nature. The felling of trees, the removal of hollow trunks, the spraying of fruit trees with poisonous solutions, the drainage of swamps and regulation of rivers—all this deprives the birds of their natural living conditions, driving many species away for good from the more densely populated regions. Similar intervention in the life of aquatic birds, such as intensified clearing of ponds and lakes and the cutting down of reeds, is responsible for the constantly diminishing numbers of these species of bird in civilised countries.

The declining numbers of birds have made naturalists and all nature lovers aware that drastic measures were needed if many species of birds were not to disappear irretrievably from civilised lands. As early as the eighteenth century various legislation was passed for the protection of the feathered community. Today, this protection of birds has been adopted by the majority of civilised countries and placed on a scientific footing. People protect the nests of songbirds from all their enemies and put up nest-boxes for those birds which otherwise nest in hollow trees.

The lack of nesting facilities is a more important factor in the driving away of birds than the presence of their natural enemies. Birds are extremely conservative as regards the choice of a nesting place and cannot usually adapt themselves to changed conditions. Those species which normally nest in hollow trees will only

7

very rarely be content with a different home. This is dependent on a number of things, such as the size of the opening, its position and height above the ground, etc. Birds nesting in bushes have their preferences for certain kinds of bush, require their nest to be at a certain height and to have, in certain cases, fallen leaves underneath it, and so on. For these reasons ornithologists from various countries have long ago agreed upon the necessary nesting conditions for the different species of birds and recommend them to all who wish to help in the task of protecting birds.

For warblers and other small birds which make their nests in bushes, it is possible to provide, in a barren corner of the garden, on a hillside or a field boundary, thickets of thorny bushes. Hawthorn, blackthorn or wild briar are best for this purpose, and they should be cut regularly so as to make them grow more thickly. A thick growth of twigs helps the birds when they build their nest and protects them from attack.

An especially acute 'housing shortage' is felt by birds nesting in holes, since a good gardener or forester will only with the greatest reluctance leave hollow trees or large trees with hollow branches in his orchard or wood. The tits, starlings, nuthatches and other birds consequently find very little suitable accommodation for their nests and very few of them are so ingenious and adaptable as some of the tits which will make do with a letter-box on a garden gate or similar 'living quarters'—even an old, discarded shoe! The majority are very choosy indeed; the starling can often be seen in the spring hopping about and inspecting a hole from every side before deciding to make his nest there. It is therefore not an easy job to make nest-boxes suitable for the different species of birds.

Nest-boxes are either made of six separate pieces of wood with a round opening in front, or drilled out of a single piece. They may have the shape of a prism, with the rear side smaller and a jutting-out roof, or some other less customary shape. The opening, however, must have an exactly suitable diameter and no light must penetrate inside save through this opening. Even when choosing a nesting place out in the open, the birds as a rule look for openings suitable to their size and only in rare cases, as with the nuthatch, are they capable of making it smaller with mud, or, like the woodpeckers, of enlarging an opening that is too small for them. The smallest diameter for the smaller tits is 1 in., for the larger ones $1^{1}/_{4}$ in., and for starlings 2 in. The boxes should be made of pieces of wood about $^{3}/_{4}$ in. thick. For tits, the bottom is usually $4^{1}/_{2}$ in. $\times$ $4^{1}/_{2}$ in., the box about 8 in. high, and the diameter of the opening varying as above. The box should be made in such a way as to make it possible to remove one of its sides for cleaning purposes.

8

The boxes should not be placed too high up on the tree, with their openings towards the east. Only the starling, whose box should measure about 6 in. × 6 in. at the bottom and be some 10 in. high, will settle in a box that is placed in a loftier position on the tree. The small tits are sometimes reluctant to make their home in openings more than 6 ft. from the ground, preferring them to be as low as possible. On the other hand it should be borne in mind that boxes placed too low are highly vulnerable, being exposed both to preying enemies and to the curiosity of children. Neither should they be placed too close together, for the insectivorous birds are big eaters and, if there were too many of them together, the birds would soon run out of food. The boxes should therefore be spaced out some 50 yards or more from each other. This, of course, does not apply to those species of birds which nest in large colonies or which fly a long way for their food. Starlings' boxes, for instance, may be placed quite close together without in any way inconveniencing the birds.

It will often be found that one or more of the boxes remain a long time without an occupant. There is a variety of possible explanations for this; the birds may not like an excess of light in the box, the positions of the box, or perhaps the fact that it is too evidently new. They prefer old, not so easily visible boxes which merge better with the surroundings.

Boxes can be made also for the redstarts and wagtails, but these should have a wide, oblong opening instead of the customary round one. These boxes are then hung up on house walls, on summer-houses, or on high garden walls. It is sometimes recommended to have the boxes built right into the wall, but according to the author's experience, only the sparrows show an interest in such boxes.

We can help house-martins to build their mud nests on the walls of our houses by placing small pieces of wood horizontally in the wall below the eaves; the birds soon realise that this is intended to give added support to their nests and they build them accordingly on top of the slats.

We can also be of assistance to thrushes, blackbirds, chaffinches and other songsters who build their nests trustingly in the fruit trees on our gardens and are thus in danger of attack by cats. This can be averted simply by placing some wire netting around the trunk of the tree to prevent the cats from climbing up. The small songsters, however, have many other enemies than cats. Thus, if we want to have these useful and attractive insect killers making their homes in our garden, we must keep magpies and jays at a respectful distance from it—otherwise they will ransack every nest in the vicinity. The shrikes present a lesser danger and will make up for their occasional misdemeanour, to which some small fledgling falls a victim, by their assiduous hunting of every kind of harmful insect. What with these and other foes—the squirrel, for example—it is something in the nature of a miracle that the defenceless nests manage to survive at all.

Throughout the cooler parts of Europe there has spread the useful habit of providing the small birds with food in wintertime. It is most frequently done in schools, where the children have special vessels and regularly fill them with something for the birds to peck. Usually they then do the same at home and are rewarded by the charming sight of various birds hopping about in the snow-covered garden or on the window-sill. These will include the tits, blackbirds, haw-finches, greenfinches, bullfinches and other small songsters. The sparrows, too, will of course take advantage of such a free meal, but there is nothing we can do about that because they are too cunning to be driven away. The food should never be placed so as to prevent the birds from seeing what is going on around them, as that would make them easy prey for cats. It is therefore advisable to place the vessel fairly high up above the ground on a bird table and in a spot that is not accessible in a single leap from the bushes or any other place of conceal-ment where an enemy might be hiding. It may be topped with a little roof to keep off the snow and to protect the feeding birds from attack by birds of prey.

Then there is the question of what food to give the birds. It is not nearly as simple a problem as it may seem. The birds' metabolism, while well able to withstand the frost and inclement weather, will not stand many foodstuffs that we eat. We must never give the birds potatoes, pastry, the remains of meals, etc. These are particularly dangerous in frosty weather as they freeze quickly and give the birds digestive troubles. They should be given only grain which is not affected by frost and is the natural food for birds, especially in winter. Dried berries, which they look for even in the open, are also suitable for many species. It is best to use a mixture of seeds such as is given to canaries: millet, sunflower seeds, oats, wheat, a little poppy seed, hemp seed, etc. Lard 'pancakes' with sunflower seeds baked in can be made for the tits and hung on the trees near the feeding place. The same can be done with raw lard, cut up into small pieces. The little winged acrobats will spend long hours fluttering about this delicacy until only the membrane will be left.

Both in summer and winter a small bird bath or drinking trough will be very welcome, especially in places where there is a lack of fresh shallow water. The birds are fond of a regular drink and bath and often find it difficult to get them, either because the water is too far away or because the banks are too steep for them. They will become used to paying regular visits to our garden to drink from and bathe in the trough and bath, particularly if these are so placed as to be out of the reach of cats. Deep basins with steep sides are extremely dangerous and many birds will drown in such a bath if there is no other water available in the neighbourhood.

Several such steps designed to make the life of the small birds easier will, in a few years, result in a noticeable increase in the number of useful songsters in our vicinity, including the rarer species which have hitherto not been seen there. If we succeed in bringing the birds into our neighbourhood and in protecting them from their enemies, they will repay us by their beautiful song and by keeping guard over our trees, which will thus at the same time be protected from insects.

The family life of birds

The bird's nest and everything connected with it can, without exaggeration, be considered to be one of the miracles of nature. It has interested ornithologists and nature lovers for many decades, and innumerable articles and books have been written about it. The remarkable composition of a bird's egg, the devoted care lavished by the parents upon the eggs, the building of the not infrequently extremely complicated nest—all this is, at first sight, so mysterious and incomprehensible that it took the scientists a long time to discover the fundamental rules governing the family life of the birds. And not even today do we know nearly all there is to know about their instincts and habits.

The bird's egg is actually one big cell covered by several different layers. Some of the eggs, as for instance the ostrich's, are very large cells indeed. The cell is formed by the germinal layer of the yolk, whereas the other parts are added later, some of them not until the egg is on its way through the oviduct.

The most interesting of the different parts of the egg is the firm outer shell, which attracts attention by its varying colouring, markings and surface structure. The shell is hard and is formed of carbonate of lime in the presence of other substances, both organic and inorganic. Before laying eggs, the birds need an adequate proportion of limy substances in their food; if kept in captivity, they must be provided with them artificially. We have all seen hens or pigeons pecking at crumbling walls or eagerly eating up eggshells that have been thrown to them. If they lack these substances, their eggs will be without a firm shell, or they may stop laying eggs altogether. A good source of carbonate of lime for cage birds is the so-called cuttle-fish bone, a limy plate found inside cephalopods, and, in particular, inside cuttle-fish.

The thickness of the bird's eggshell varies, depending both on the species of bird and on the environment in which the eggs are laid. The strongest shell is usually possessed by the eggs of birds nesting in open nests on the ground, the thinnest in the case of birds that make their nests in hollows or strongly knit nests. The inner tension of the contents adds a certain firmness to the egg, too. All eggshells, without exception, are thoroughly porous to enable the embryo to breathe properly. If the shell of an egg is painted over with some non-porous material, the embryo inside will quickly suffocate. The surface structure of the shell—a very striking feature in the case of some species of birds—is, to a certain extent, connected with its porousness.

Birds' eggs have a distinctive beauty of their own. There are eggs white as snow, yellowish eggs resembling ivory, eggs of azure, greenish, pinkish, coffee brown, almost black, and other hues; eggs of a single colour and many-coloured ones with rich ornamentation. Some have a design of spots or hair-lines, others large blotches of different colours. Why this lavishness of colour in the case of some species, while other have plain, one-coloured or even completely white eggs? It is nature's camouflage, just as in the colouring of the bird's feathers, the mammal's skin or the scales of fish. A nest full of motley coloured and ornamented eggs is less conspicuous in the open and is therefore safer from enemies. In some cases the camouflage is so perfect that the nest will not be seen even at close quarters; the eggs of some marsh birds, for instance, merge so well with their surroundings that one steps on the nest before one notices it. White eggs are laid by birds nesting in dark hollows or in deep nests where no camouflage is necessary. Also the strong and fearless birds, such as some birds of prey and storks, who know how to defend their nests from any attack, usually have white eggs.

The egg is coloured by substances supplied by the oviduct, in particular red and blue, apart from various mixtures and combinations. The basic colour of the shell is usually characteristic for a particular species of bird, but some birds lay eggs of varying colours, so that, for instance, gulls frequently have eggs ranging in colour from green to brown in a variety of hues. In the case of some songsters, the eggs of the first lay differ in colour from those of the second, while cuckoos have eggs similar to those of the 'host' in whose nest they are used to laying them.

The shape of the egg, too, is characteristic for the various species and groups of birds. What might be called the standard type of egg is that laid by the domestic hen and by the majority of other birds. The plovers and some of the gulls have markedly pointed eggs, some ducks and divers have very elongated ones, while those of owls and birds of prey are, on the contrary, almost round. The size and weight of eggs in the majority of species are extremely constant, and average sizes and weights can be given when describing the different species. Exceptionally large eggs, out of all proportion to their own size, are laid by the exotic kiwis and megapodes. The cuckoo, on the other hand, has relatively small eggs. There is a wide range of sizes, from the pea-like eggs of the humming-birds to the huge ones of the ostrich family.

Before they build their nests and lay eggs, the birds go through a hectic and complicated period of courtship during which the males try to attract the females and win their favour. Usually the males, at this time, have very brightly coloured and shiny feathers and various ornaments such as combs and other protuberances on their heads or spurs on their feet. They may have all kinds of tufts, bonnets, pendants, tail fans, elongated feathers, colourful patches in the wings and other ornaments, distinguishing them sharply from their plain, non-descript mates. They preen themselves, hop and dance about, stretch their necks and bow, spread and again fold their tail fans and their wings in an endeavour to attract the attention of the females. Only very rarely are both sexes of the same colour; there is no difference in the appearance of male and female storks, herons, some of the birds of prey, the owls and a few of the songsters. The finery, however, has only been lent to the male for the time of courtship, after which he has to change into more simple workaday clothing. Sometimes the change is very striking indeed, and it almost looks as though the male bird were ashamed of his ordinary appearance. This impression is particularly vivid in the case of the wild drakes which can be seen wandering around singly through the reed-beds in their greyish-brown summer clothing.

The relation of the male and female phalarope is completely reversed, the male being inconspicuously coloured, incubating the eggs, teaching the young and relying on the protection of his stronger mate. She, for her part, is beautifully coloured, and once she has laid the eggs, does nothing but fight with her neighbours.

The two sexes often also differ in size. Male cocks, ostriches, swans, geese, ducks and some of the songsters are considerably larger than their mates—they have longer wings, legs, beaks and tail feathers, etc. In some cases, however, it is the other way round, the female bird being appreciably larger than the male. This is especially noticeable with the birds of prey; the female hawks and sparrow-hawks, in particular, are surprisingly bigger and sturdier than their mates.

The voice of the majority of male birds likewise distinguishes them from the females, being far louder and more melodious. Sometimes, indeed, it is complete-ly different, as in the case of the cocks of our domestic hens, of the nightingales, and of the cuckoo. The females of these species make completely different sounds from those of the males. Bird song is very closely linked with the function of the sex glands—if they are more developed, it is stronger, if less developed, weaker. This can well be noticed in early spring, or in the case of young male birds whose typical male voice first sounds softly, almost timidly, before it gains its full volume. Although each species has its own characteristic type of voice, there are variations inside the species, so that, for instance, in the case of songsters we find master singers with beautiful voices and a broad range, as well as mere dilettantes having a very limited repertoire. This is well known to all who keep songbirds, their aim always being to obtain the best performers for their cages.

The 'marriage' which follows the hectic and frequently highly belligerent mating period takes the most varied forms and is of varying durability: there are species, such as the pigeons, the big birds of prey, the storks and some others, which strike up lasting partnerships, the two birds showing each other the same affection as a pair of human lovers. If separated for a time, the birds return to each other again; they keep together even out of the nesting season, and will make their nest together regularly every year, usually in the same neighbourhood, or even in exactly the same spot. Although fairly rare, there are cases known in which, after the death of its mate, the surviving bird will remain alone without a new partner. Other birds, as for instance our songsters, take partners only for the nesting period, as a rule a different partner every year. During the nesting period, however, they too stay faithfully together, feed each other, defend each other from enemies, and altogether give the impression of being a happy and orderly married couple. Birds like our domestic cocks, on the other hand, are confirmed polygamists, a single cock having a whole harem of hens of whom, as well as of the chickens, he takes not the slightest notice, his only interests being to make love and to fight with the other roosters. Curious also is the behaviour of the cuckoo; she is always surrounded by a number of males, with whom she mates without any system whatever. Otherwise, every cuckoo, male as well as female, lives on its own without the least regard for others of the species. Some birds make their nests in large colonies, close to one another and constantly full of noise and altercation, while others seek the most secluded and quiet spots in which to rear a family. It should be borne in mind, however, that these differences are not due to the will of the individual but to the ecological characteristics of each species, just as are the bird's other actions—mode of life, the kind of food it eats, the way it sings, etc. It is thus almost impossible for any single individual of a species to live in any other way than that prescribed for it by nature.

As soon as they start wooing, the birds will begin to look round for a suitable place in which to build their nest. The different, and often highly ingenious, methods of nest-building are again part of the ecological characteristics of the respective species; the birds make their nests quite instinctively, guided by an inborn sense, in a place natural to their species, using a certain material, giving

14

the nest a certain shape that is characteristic for the species, lining it in a typical way. In short, the building, placing and shape of the nest are all ecological characteristics of the species from which the bird cannot and does not deviate. That means that the birds do not have to learn how to build their nest, which explains why birds kept in captivity from their birth will, when the time comes, build a nest exactly as do the other members of their species, though they have never seen it done before.

A bird's nest is nothing short of a small miracle. There are innumerable different types of nests, from the simple scooped-out hollow in the ground to the artistically executed nest of the warbler and the mud creations of the swallows and oven-birds. There are nests among the tops of tall conifers, deep inside hollows in tree-trunks, nests in dark caves, in underground burrows and dens, underneath heaps of stone and in stacks of wood, among reeds, or again floating on the surface of the water. There are nests made of moss, hay, hair, twigs and pieces of wood, of mud or clay, and even of the saliva of the birds themselves. It would take a whole book to describe all the different types of nests that exist. In every case, however, whatever its shape or location, the nest is a comfortable and cosy place for the young fledglings. According to the type of nest, it is easily possible to tell what species of bird it belongs to; only the cuckoo does not bother to build a nest of its own, but leaves the care of its young to foster-parents.

When all the eggs have been laid in the nest, it is necessary to hatch them out—and that is a very difficult thing indeed for the restless, lively birds. The number of eggs, by the way, may vary, according to the species, from one to twenty. Birds have a higher body temperature than mammals, and at this time their temperature further increases, so that a sitting bird often behaves as though it had fever. This can be most easily observed in the case of a domestic hen. The heat is essential to bring the embryo inside the egg to life and to help it grow. The birds warm the eggs with their naked bodies; they have bare spots on their breasts which are normally covered by feathers. When sitting down on top of the eggs, the bird will spread aside these feathers to bring the eggs into direct contact with its skin. For hatching purposes the eggs also require a certain moisture which they receive through morning dew and rain, as well as from the bird's body, as it often comes to the nest wet all over. Long before humans thought of artificial hatching in incubators, the Australian megapodes used this method to hatch their eggs, placing them among poles of fallen leaves to be hatched without the parents' assistance. The heat produced by the decaying vegetable matter is sufficient to hatch out the eggs. A similar method is practised by snakes and lizards.

The eggs are hatched either by both parents in turn, or by the female only. There are cases, however, such as the phalarope and the emu, where the males take over this responsibility. Sometimes the way the birds take turns is extremely interesting; for instance male African ostriches, which are black in colour, sit on the eggs at night, while the brown females do so in the daytime. In the case of the majority of songsters the males and females both take turns in hatching the eggs, though some, such as the canaries, leave it solely to the females.

The birds usually feed one another while they are sitting on the eggs. Especially curious in this respect are the exotic hornbills—the male 'walls up' the female in a tree hollow in such a way that only the tip of her beak protrudes, and then feeds both her and the fledglings until they are ready to come out.

The time needed for the embryo to be hatched differs according to the size and species of the birds, being eleven days in the case of the smallest birds and up to six weeks in the case of the ostriches. Not even all the eggs in one nest will hatch out at one and the same time, and there may be a time lag of as much as a week or more between the first and the last to be hatched. This happens whenever the adult birds sit on the eggs directly the first one is laid; we then find that next to newborn, naked fledglings, there are, in the nest, also some slightly older ones which already have feathers. The owls and herons are good examples of this phenomenon. As a rule, however, the birds do not sit on the eggs before they have all been laid, so that, consequently, all the young will be hatched in one day. This is especially the case with the songsters.

The fledgling has to work very hard in order to see the light of day, for it is no easy task to peck its way through the often extremely hard shell. It uses a special hard, sharp tooth which the newly hatched fledgling has on the tip of its beak and which gradually disappears until, a few days later, no trace of it is left. The struggle to get out of the egg is an extremely strenuous one, and so the little bird takes a rest every now and then before continuing its attack on the shell. Sometimes the mother bird will take a hand—or rather a beak—in the matter, helping the fledgling from the outside, but only very cautiously since she might easily hurt the soft body which is, as it were, stuck on to the inside of the shell.

The newly hatched birds differ considerably in the stage of development in which they arrive in this world; while the young of geese, ducks and similar birds come out of the egg already 'equipped' with a fine, thick coat and are fairly independent right from their birth, the fledglings of the birds of prey, owls, songsters and some others are helpless little creatures, often mere blind embryos, which take a long time to grow to be like birds and to look out at the world. They require even longer before they can stand on their own feet and sally forth out of the nest. In the first case, that is in the case of the more developed and independent fledglings, they will soon seek their own food, while in the case of the others, they have to be fed for a considerable time by their parents, who bring them the food and in some species, such as pigeons, partially digest it in their crops before giving it to their young. It is interesting to note that the birds often give their young quite different food from that which they are in the habit of eating themselves. Thus, for instance, sparrows and other birds that live on seeds, at first feed their young with insects. The fledglings consume surprising quantities of food, so that a nest of insectivorous birds represents a considerable insect-destroying element in the orchard or countryside.

The parent birds defend their young with admirable fearlessness against every danger, be it rain, wind, hail, the rays of the sun, the cold, or any live enemy. They protect the fledglings from the rain or hail by spreading their feathers over the nest or over the young birds themselves if they happen to be out of the nest, and cases are known of female birds being killed by hailstones while shielding their offspring in this way. If danger threatens from some live enemy, they will actively defend their nest and their young, even against obviously hopeless odds. And not infrequently they will succeed in scaring away the foe merely by their desperate courage. Some birds make use of instinctive subterfuge to lure the enemy away from their nest or from their brood of fledglings. Bird-watchers and naturalists often witness the touching spectacle of a partridge mother fluttering about in the field as though she were wounded just to distract attention from her nest, and then quickly returning to it in a wide arc. A similar trick was once played on the author by a female rock partridge in the mountains of Crete; only after he had followed her about for some time did he succeed in finding, well concealed among the rocks, her nest with the striped fledglings. The birds frequently use this manoeuvre, both against human beings and against the beasts of prey. The stronger and more belligerent birds are naturally far more likely to succeed in the defence of their progeny; both men and dogs in the frozen North know very well that it is better to keep away from the nests of the wild swan, the male swans being extremely formidable opponents. With their broad and strong wings they will drive away every foe, and people are known to have drowned as a result of such a fierce attack by nesting swans. But one need not go so far to see how the adult birds defend their offspring—just try to take a little chick away from an ordinary domestic hen, or a fluffy yellow gosling from its vigilant mother! Other birds, such as gulls, which nest in large colonies, will join forces and defend their young together. Swallows, too, can often be seen driving a bird of prey away from their nest, or small kestrels attacking a clumsy buzzard.

Nature lovers are often puzzled by the question as to whether birds teach their young anything for use in their later life. True, many of the actions and habits that an adult bird acquires are of a purely instinctive character and do not have to be learned. Such is, for instance, swimming in the case of the aquatic species, diving, flying and, as mentioned earlier, nest-building and other aspects of family life. Nevertheless, it does sometimes seem that there are certain things which the young bird is taught by its elders, or that at least it perfects itself in some activity, thanks to the example of the parents. In the mountains it is possible to watch for several hours at a time how a family of eagles play with a dead animal that the parents have brought to the nest. The old birds fly up repeatedly, high into the air, and drop the prey among the eaglets circling beneath them, which then dive to seize it. Starlings and shrikes learn all the time to improve their song, adding ever new trills and widening their vocal range, while those who keep canaries know that a young canary learns best from a good adult performer.

Among the unsolved mysteries of nature is the mutual recognition of birds belonging to one family. It is a well known fact that the sense of smell plays a very inferior part with the birds, and it is of no consequence as regards our present problem. Yet the fact remains that a hen will unerringly distinguish her chickens from others of exactly the same age, even if they happen to belong to the same race. However puzzling it may be to us, it would seem that the birds can distinguish each other by appearance.

PLATES

The kestrel

(Falco tinnunculus L.)

The kestrel is a familiar and beneficial bird of prey, frequenting woodland, moor, marsh and coast. Many people call it *Wind-hover*, because of the way it hovers, practically immobile in the air, keenly scrutinising the ground for any sign of animal life. It is one of the smaller members of the falcon tribe, birds traditionally owned and trained for hunting by royalty and nobility. It has powerful, pointed wings, with which it is capable of attaining great speeds (it is estimated to exceed 100 m.p.h. at times), a short neck, and the short, hooked beak of all birds of prey.

The kestrel's flight is relaxed and leisurely as a rule, and when hunting it will glide and hover twenty to thirty feet above ground level. When the prey is sighted the kestrel swoops, despatching its victim rapidly with claws and beak. Mammals are particularly sought after, including rats, fieldmice, shrews, voles, frogs and small birds; domestic fowl are generally left alone. Like the owls, it ejects stomach castings in pellet form. It is a shameful fact, however, that this enemy of vermin should be shot, even today, as if it were a common game bird.

Although not more than fourteen inches in length, the kestrel is a compact and handsome bird. The adult male has a bluish-grey head, rump and tail, the last with a broad, black band; the upper parts are chestnut-brown spotted with black, the under parts buff, streaked and spotted black. The female is rufous-brown, with a barred tail, and slightly larger than the male.

The kestrel builds no nest, but lays its eggs, four or five in number, in hollow tree-trunks, disused nests or on ledges of cliffs. The male is responsible for catching the food, the female feeding it to the young birds, who remain in the nest for four or five weeks. Instances have been recorded of kestrels breeding on roofs of houses and public buildings in large cities.

Among other names given to this bird are *Stannel*, *Red Hawk* and *Wind-fanner*. Its relatives include the lesser kestrel and the red-footed falcon.

The common buzzard

(Buteo buteo L.*)*

The common buzzard is larger than the kestrel, averaging over twenty inches in length, and can be found in most parts of Europe and throughout the British Isles. It has, however, been widely persecuted over the years. In Ireland, for example, the species was practically exterminated late in the nineteenth century; and even today, mistaken perhaps with its great wide wings for the golden eagle, though considerably smaller, it is often the victim of the sportsman's gun. Partly as a result, the buzzard shuns populated areas, preferring solitary rugged coasts, bleak moors and mountains.

Unlike the kestrel, it was never highly favoured as a hunting bird, lacking both its speed and intelligence. It preys on all kinds of small mammals, including many harmful rodents. Young rabbits, mice, rats, reptiles, small birds and insects are all fair game, but the amount of food which the male buzzard brings to its nest is often far more than the fledglings can possibly consume. All prey is captured on the ground.

The buzzard is almost entirely brown in colour, though the shades are much varied, ranging from white with brown spots and bars to a uniform brown mantle with mottled brown and white under parts. It has tremendous powers of concentration and endurance, its hunting methods being similar to those of other hawks, although it will only hover for short periods. More typical is its noble, spiralling flight and wide-circling glide, with wings taut and tail extended. The rounded wings clearly distinguish the bird in flight, and at times it will soar almost beyond the range of the eye. One might expect such a bird to utter a fierce, challenging call, but its most characteristic note is a plaintive mewing, especially when its nest is approached.

The buzzard's nest is a bulky affair of boughs and sticks, lined with grass, moss, leaves and occasional bits of heather or seaweed. The two or three eggs are greenish-white, with blotches of red or brown.

Little Eagle, Black Kite and *Glider* are some other names given to this bird, who is, on the whole, a good friend to man.

The barn owl

(Tyto alba Scop.)

Owls have figured prominently in the folk-lore, myths and legends of many races, and have habitually been regarded as birds of ill-omen. The barn owl, with its ghostly silhouette and uncanny, piercing shriek has struck fear into the hearts of successive generations of superstitious country folk, although, in truth, its evil reputation is utterly undeserved. It preys relentlessly on rodents and crop-destroying mammals and is thus a valuable ally to the farmer.

The barn owl has a white, heart-shaped face with a tawny brown ruff. The under parts are also white, the rest of its plumage being golden brown. Its strong bill is almost concealed beneath a double ridge of feathers, and the overall softness of the plumage renders the bird's slow, powerful flight completely noiseless.

It flies at dusk, resting and sleeping by day. Its favourite roosting places are in barns, church-towers, ruins and tree hollows. These are also its chosen breeding places, the pure white eggs being deposited on castings and decayed wood, with no attempt made to build a proper nest. In common with most owls, the mates are loyal to one another for long periods, often for life.

The owl's remarkable nocturnal powers of detection enable it to locate its prey even in pitch darkness. When captured, the creature is either swallowed whole or carried back to the owl's regular night-time station, there to be stored or eaten later. The indigestible parts are regurgitated in the form of small blackish pellets.

In addition to its shriek, which caused Lady Macbeth to refer to it as 'the fatal bellman, which gives the stern'st good-night,' the barn owl has a repertory of chirruping, hissing and snorting sounds, which have earned it such local names as *Screech Owl, Hissing Owl* and *Roarer*. Elsewhere it is known as *Billy Wise,* and Tennyson was doubtless alluding to this side of its nature when he wrote,

> 'Alone and warming his five wits,
> The white owl in the belfry sits.'

24

The tawny owl

(Strix aluco L.*)*

The tamest and most thoroughly nocturnal of British owls is the tawny, wood or brown owl, to give three variations of its name. Confined to the woods by day, it emerges towards dusk to set up night stations on open ground, from which vantage points it ranges deliberately and noiselessly over the countryside in search of young rabbits, voles, field-mice, moles and other small animals. It is also partial to young birds and is known to eat fish as well.

The tawny owl, as its name implies, is brownish in colour, mottled and streaked all over, with barred wings and tail. It has the familiar large round head and flattened face, with deep-set, penetrating eyes. The neck, hidden by the thick soft plumage, is capable of swivelling the head almost back to front, so that a wide area can be surveyed without the necessity of a change in the position of the body. Powerful legs and sharp talons render it a formidable adversary, and an intruder will often retire severely injured as a result. The prey is snatched without warning from the ground and if not immediately eaten, taken back to the owl's station, the site of which is often betrayed by the ejected pellets. Small birds are often attacked while roosting, the owl flapping its wings against the bushes to frighten them out.

Nesting habits are variable, any opening or deserted nest serving the purpose; even rabbit holes and squirrels' dreys are used. The eggs are large and white, like the barn owl's, and the newly-born fledglings are covered with thick white down.

This is the traditional 'hooting' owl, probably the one mentioned by Shakespeare as 'the staring owl that nightly sings tu-whit, tu-whoo, a merry note.' In addition to this hooting, only heard at dusk and at night, the tawny owl emits a cacophony of screams, gurgles, coughs, snores and whistles, so that Shakespeare is again accurate in describing him as 'the clamorous owl, that nightly hoots.' Other familiar nicknames include *Billy Hooter* and *Ferny Hoolet.*

The little owl

(Athene noctua L.)

This owl, about nine inches in length and therefore not much larger than a blackbird, was introduced to Britain from Holland as recently as 1889. It was then known as the 'fierce little foreigner' and is today referred to as the *Dutch Owl, Belgian Owl, French Owl* and even *Spanish Owl*. It now nests freely throughout central and southern England.

It is, indeed, a fierce and daring bird, tackling animals and birds of its own size in addition to the normal owl diet of small mammals, beetles, caterpillars, spiders and other insects. It is not exclusively nocturnal in habit although most of its hunting is done by night. Even in broad daylight it may be seen perched erect on a branch, hedge or gate, where thus exposed it will sometimes be attacked by hordes of other birds who are not deceived by its diminutive size.

The little owl has a small flat head, greyish-brown upper parts spotted and mottled with white, whitish under parts streaked with brown, white bars on wings and tail, and grey legs and toes, covered with bristles. It has a loud, monotonous, sharp call-note, interspersed with a curious cat-like mewing. For a nesting place it will select any crevice or hollow in a tree, wall or rock, with no special nesting material. The eggs, four or five in number, and dull white in colour, may even be laid on the ground. Fledglings are covered with a creamy down which later changes to reddish-grey.

The little owl is often held responsible for the destruction of eggs and young game birds, although examination of its pellets has proved the accusation unfounded. It has played its part in superstition and folk-lore, and was the owl consecrated to the Greek goddess Athene, as its Latin name implies. She was originally a war deity but was also worshipped as the goddess of the arts of peace and goddess of intelligence. Athene took the owl as her emblem, and its image was stamped on a number of silver coins. The bird was thus universally revered in Greece, though the Romans later regarded it as a bird of ill-omen.

The long-eared owl

(Asio otus L.)

The long-eared owl, also known variously as the *Horned Owl* or *Tufted Owl*, is so called because of the two ear-tufts on its head, which can be raised at will. It is a fierce-looking bird, the female being slightly larger than the male. The upper parts are buff, mottled and streaked with grey and brown; the under parts are grey and buff, with dark cross and arrow-like markings. The facial disk is pale buff and is encircled by a white ruff edged with black; the eyes are surrounded by a blackish band. The colour of the iris is orange-yellow, another distinguishing feature from other owls, who have yellow irides. Legs and toes are covered with light brown feathers.

The long-eared owl preys on vermin, on insects of all kinds and on small birds. Examination of its pellets show that birds form a fairly substantial part of the diet. It is a nocturnal bird and during the day perches in a tree, its body pressed tightly against the trunk for concealment. If detected by day it will be mobbed furiously by smaller birds. It is one of the quieter members of the owl family, its flight being typically silent and its calls and cries infrequent. The normal cry is a protracted, plaintive, wavering note, and it is reported to emit mewing and barking noises as well. During courtship, or when angered, the male bird will sometimes clap its wings, producing a sharp cracking sound.

The long-eared owl may be found in all wooded districts, but is especially fond of fir-woods. It chooses the deserted nests of other birds to lay its white eggs, four to six in number; among the nests selected are those of the jay, the magpie, the wood-pigeon, the crow and the sparrow-hawk. Sometimes a squirrel's drey is used, and occasionally the eggs are laid on the bare ground.

The bird has more migratory habits than most other owls. It moves about quite freely during the autumn, when it is joined by visitors from overseas. Its fierce attitude and habits have given rise to much superstition and legend, mostly of an adverse nature.

The cuckoo

(Cuculus canorus L.*)*

Although much celebrated in legend, verse and song, and generally welcomed as one of the messengers of spring, the cuckoo has a number of unendearing habits, and is not popular with other birds. It builds no nest of its own, but blending opportunism and guile, deposits its eggs in the nests of other species, who promptly rear the baby cuckoos as their own. If necessary, eggs which are already lying in the selected nest are removed, then destroyed or swallowed whole.

Compared with the size of the mother bird—about thirteen inches long—the cuckoo's eggs are small, the colour varying from white to green or buff, and often similar to the eggs of the chosen host. The newly-hatched cuckoo will show no gratitude either to its foster-mother or her brood. Unhatched eggs will be hoisted on to its broad back and tumbled out of the nest. Apparently unsuspecting, the foster-mother will continue to feed the young cuckoo, which already dwarfs her in size, until long after it is able to fly.

Among more than one hundred species chosen for this unrewarding work are the meadow pipit, hedge sparrow, robin, reed warbler and yellow wagtail. The Fool, in Shakespeare's *King Lear*, remarks,

'The hedge sparrow fed the cuckoo so long,

That it had it head bit off by it young.'

The cuckoo, nevertheless, has its useful side, as it consumes many harmful insects, including hairy ones rejected by all other birds. Its predominating colour is slate-grey, the under parts being whitish and darkly barred. The name is derived from the familiar, melodious call of the male; the call of the female is a bubbling sound, rarely heard. The bird is a summer visitor to the British Isles, wintering in Africa. The adult birds frequently leave the country some weeks before their young, who experience little difficulty in finding their own way to winter quarters. They are strong fliers, and on the wing may easily be mistaken for sparrowhawks.

The nightjar

(Caprimulgus europaeus L.*)*

Unusual both in appearance and habits, the nightjar is a summer resident in Britain, a frequenter of woods, heath and moorland. It is a sturdy bird, greyish-brown in colour, with black, buff and chestnut streaks, the male having white tips to the outer tail feathers. The general effect is to camouflage the bird completely in its woodland haunts. The bird has a flat head, small bill and huge, bristled mouth. Its legs are short and the middle claw is notched like a comb.

The nightjar, like the owls, spends most of the day resting, either on a low branch or on the ground. Its favourite perch is lengthwise along the branch, head resting on breast. At twilight it emerges, gliding silently over the tree tops on long extended wings, twisting and wheeling in its hunt for insects, mostly harmful ones, which form its entire diet.

Equally unusual are the nightjar's breeding habits. No nest whatsoever is built, two eggs being laid on the bare ground, close to bracken. The greyish-white eggs are difficult to detect and far less conspicuous than if some form of nesting material were employed. The young, when hatched, are naked and blind, but with the protective colouring of the parents, to guard against marauders. If surprised, they will instinctively turn on their backs and hiss, and this sound may account for the bird being popularly believed to be harmful and malevolent.

Most of the nicknames for this bird are uncomplimentary, such as *Night-hawk*, *Puck Bird*, *Scissors Grinder*, *Flying Toad* and *Goatsucker*. The last name, which is also its Latin family title, is derived from the ancient supposition that the bird sucked the udders of she-goats, resulting, in some illogical way, in the eventual blindness of the animal. Furthermore, its habit of opening its ugly mouth wide to warn off assailants is hardly likely to endear it to sentimental bird lovers.

The nightjar's song is a weird, undulating trill, which is sometimes accompanied by the violent clapping of wings over the back in sharp, pistol-like reports.

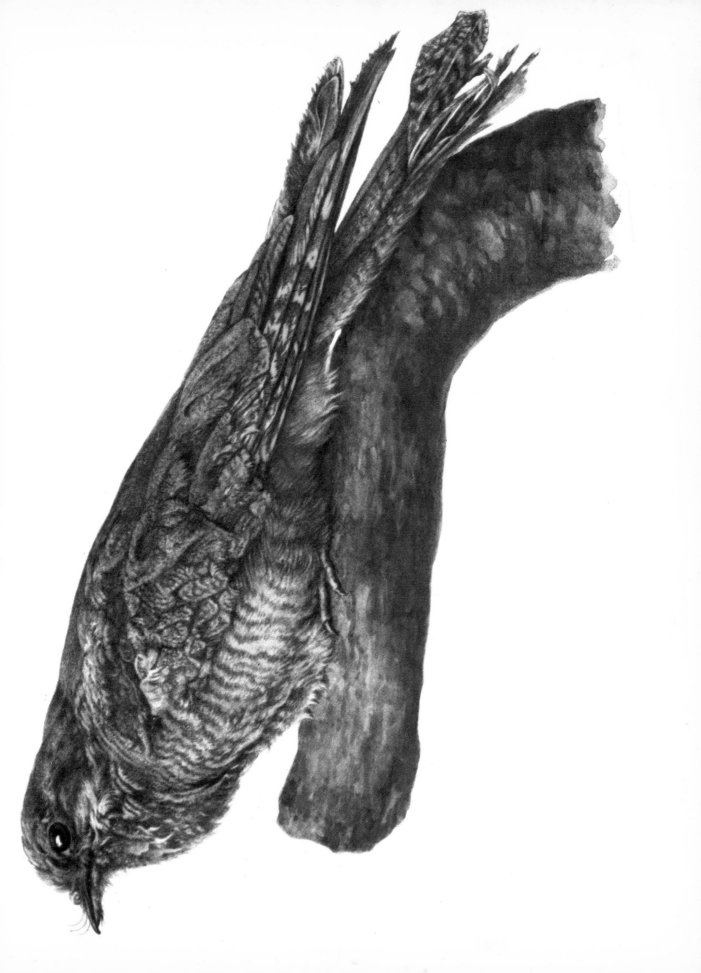

The swift

(Apus apus L.*)*

The swift is, as its name implies, one of the speed champions of the bird kingdom. Although similar in habit and appearance, it is not related to the swallow, but to the humming-bird, who is the only bird of its size who can outstrip it in speed. The swift is only about seven inches long, and its sickle-shaped wings are as long as the body. The tail is short and not markedly forked, the beak is small and sharply hooked, the legs are uselessly short and weak. Its predominating colour is dark brown, and there is a distinguishing white patch on the throat.

Although much seen in gardens and frequently making its nest in rafters, the swift is not a very friendly bird, and its feeding habits are completely independent. Its food consists exclusively of insects caught on the wing. The swift's body construction fits it for an almost entirely aerial existence, and it is thrilling to watch hundreds of these graceful birds soaring, gliding, diving and spiralling high in the air on a summer evening. It has been rumoured, though not verified, that the bird is even able to sleep aloft at considerable heights. So ill-adapted are the swift's legs for life on the ground that if by mischance it does alight on level terrain it has the greatest difficulty in taking off again. In fact, legend has it that the bird is quite unable to stand upright.

The swift's nesting material is also taken in flight. The nest is a flimsy affair, made of scraps of straw and feathers, all cemented with saliva, and affixed to a suitable vertical surface. Any hole or crevice will suffice, and they nest, as they fly, in large colonies. The two or three eggs are dull white and elongated in shape, and the young birds may be confined to the nest for as long as six weeks. They are quick learners, however, and when they finally leave the nest, are soon able to join the adult birds as they flock, screaming shrilly, in preparation for the long southward migration. They are already on their way in August, earlier than most other summer guests, to South Africa and neighbouring warm lands.

The kingfisher

(Alcedo atthis L.)

The kingfisher is the most brilliantly and gorgeously coloured of all British birds. Its Greek name is 'Halcyon', and a bird of this name, according to legend, used to breed in nests on the crest of the waves, charming the winds and calming the sea. Thus the bird was popularly associated with calm, peace and happy portent.

It is a small bird, about seven and a half inches long, with a disproportionately large head, short tail, and long black dagger-like bill. Its back, wings and tail are cobalt-blue, but may in certain lights appear emerald-green. The under parts are russet-brown, throat and neck patched white, feet red. There is little variation between the bird's summer and winter plumage.

The kingfisher is a surprisingly agile flier, and is nearly always seen near to water, especially slow-flowing rivers and streams, ponds and brooks. It perches on a branch overhanging the water, or even hovers directly over it, plunging down in a spectacular dive at the merest hint of movement. Its favourite types of fish are minnows and stickle-backs, and it also hunts for aquatic insects. Returning to its perch, it swallows the fish head first, tossing it into the air if necessary to get it into the correct position. In the winter it may stray to the sea-shore in search of small crustaceans.

The kingfisher's nest is generally found in mud banks or occasionally in sandpits. A long horizontal tunnel is bored into the bank by both birds. This extends for two or three feet and ends in a rounded chamber, in which the eggs are deposited, six or seven in number, spherical and glossy white. They are usually hemmed in by a pile of undigested fishbones, which renders the atmosphere somewhat unpleasant. The young birds are born naked, but soon develop a bristle-like sheath, which then peels off to reveal the gaudy plumage of the adult. The fledglings are fed by both parents, instinctively forming a circular queue at the base of the tunnel, and applying one by one for their meal.

The hoopoe

(Upupa epops L.*)*

The hoopoe is a common bird on the Continent, but is rarely seen in Britain. It does, however, occasionally breed in the southern English counties, and has been spotted in parks and gardens. When seen, and its arboreal habits make this seldom, it is unmistakable. The adult male has a conspicuous fan-shaped crest and a long slender bill. Its plumage is fawn, with black tips to the crest, and with alternating, zebra-like black and white bars on wings and tail. The under parts are white. As with so many exotic birds, the female is smaller and plainer.

The bird is closely related to the hornbill, and derives its name from the 'poo-poo-poo' call note which it utters, the neck feathers being puffed out after each triple cry. If singing perched, the hoopoe jerks its head skyward, but if on the ground, drives its long bill into the earth.

It is an expert fly-catcher and also eats larger insects when locally available, such as grasshoppers and locusts. These are often rapped against a hard surface or tossed in the air before being swallowed. As the beak probes the soil for insects, the crest is folded back out of the way.

Hoopoes are solitary birds and travel about either alone or in pairs. They breed in wooded and well-watered districts, in holes, ant-hills, or low down in trees. The nest is unambitious, merely a few chips or dead leaves, generally mixed with animal excrement, which habit has earned the bird the name of *Dung Bird*. Four to eight pale blue or white eggs are laid, both parents feeding the young birds, and the male taking over completely a week or so after hatching. The young are born naked but rapidly acquire a layer of down and a set of sharp quills.

The hoopoe has featured prominently in legend and was supposed to have assisted Solomon in building the Temple. The Arabs have held it in special reverence, believing it to possess medicinal properties as well as powers of water-divining.

40

The green woodpecker

(Picus viridis L.*)*

The green woodpecker is the largest of the three common British varieties. It is a handsome, distinctively-coloured bird with its crimson head and green and gold plumage. The upper parts are dark, the under parts greyish-green, the rump yellow. Nape and crown are vivid crimson, the tail black, with green bars. The adult male also has a black patch over the eye region and a crimson moustache-like stripe; in the female this stripe is black.

Like all woodpeckers, the green variety is sturdily built and has a powerful, pointed bill. As its name implies, it is a woodland dweller, though frequently extending its range to parks, orchards and gardens. It feeds mainly on insects, which it seeks in the trunks and branches of trees, particularly where the wood has rotted. The bird ascends the vertical tree-trunk in a series of jerky hops, its body pressed close to the trunk, tapping at intervals on the bark. Immediately something of interest is located, it bores a hole, darts out a long, sticky tongue, and devours its victim. Similar methods are adopted on the ground, particularly on ant-hills, and the diet is freely augmented with seeds, grain and berries.

The woodpecker's nest, if it can so be termed, is merely a hole drilled into the tree trunk. The entrance is narrow, and a passage then descends perpendicularly for about a foot. At the base of this passage the eggs are laid, no nesting material being added save a few wood chips. It is small wonder that woodpecker nests are seldom explored. The eggs are pointed and translucent, frequently stained brown or yellow by tree secretions. The baby birds are fed with regurgitated food, in milky paste form.

The green woodpecker has no characteristic song, but can be recognised by a loud, laughing sound which has resulted in the bird being known locally as the *Yaffle*. Other more obvious nicknames are *Cutbill*, *Hew-hole* and *Nicker-pecker*.

42

The great spotted woodpecker

(Dendrocopus major L.)

This is the least common of the three well-known types of woodpecker, smaller than the green and larger than the lesser spotted variety. Like the others, it is a resident in Britain, and is distributed fairly evenly throughout the country, though barely a hundred years ago extinct in Scotland. It lives in woods and copses, but is not such a frequent visitor to parks and gardens.

It is a striking black and white bird, back and crown being black, the sides of the face white with black markings. The male has a crimson patch on the neck. Wings are barred black and white, the under parts being dull buff. Belly and under tail coverts are red, shoulder patches white. It has the typical woodpecker's toe formation, two pointing backwards and two forwards. This formation helps the bird to retain its upright position on the tree and assists it in climbing.

The habits and diet of the great spotted woodpecker are similar to those of its green cousin. It lives chiefly on insects, and seems to know instinctively where tell-tale decayed wood can be found. It can be recognised, however, by the 'drumming' sound emitted by both sexes. This is caused by loud, vibrating, rapidly-produced blows of the bill, audible for considerable distances, and probably employed as call signals. It is not, as sometimes believed, vocally produced, and is generally heard during the breeding season.

Its nesting habits are also similar to those of the green woodpecker, though the hole is usually bored at a higher level. The young, moreover, are fed from the beak. The eggs are creamy-white, five to seven in all.

Since little reliance is placed upon feeding at ground level, this woodpecker, like many other mainly arboreal birds, suffers acutely in severe cold weather, when frozen bark prevents it from obtaining a normal supply of insects.

Woodpeckers have, at various times and places, been objects of worship. The Greeks identified them with Zeus, the Romans with Mars. In many countries they are also revered as rain gods.

The lesser spotted woodpecker

(Dendrocopus minor L.)

The lesser spotted or barred woodpecker is only five to six inches long, about the size of a sparrow. Although it is quite common in Britain, particularly in the southern half, it is not often seen because of its shy nature. It is a most attractive little bird and well deserving of protection. It frequents every type of woodland, parkland and orchard, spending most of its time at the top of the tallest available tree and rarely venturing far from cover. The adult male has a crimson crown, buff forehead, white ear coverts, black nape and black moustachial stripe; the female's crown is white, that of the fledgling also crimson. The upper parts are black with distinctive white bars, the under parts white with black streaks on the flanks. Both wings and outer tail feathers are also barred. The bill and the legs are slate-grey.

Its habits and food requirements are similar to those of the great spotted woodpecker —mostly insects and harmful grubs and larvae. It does not, however, feed so liberally on fruit and nuts. Despite its relatively small size it is as expert and energetic in boring holes as are its larger relatives. Like them, the lesser spotted woodpecker only goes to work on trees which are already infected by insects, and a litter of chips at the base of a tree is a certain guide to its activity. Its nest is generally found some distance up the tree, sometimes thirty or forty feet from the ground; it consists of the familiar horizontal tunnel, descending into a wider chamber in which are deposited between five and eight glossy pure white eggs, usually on a thin layer of wood chips.

The sound made by the barred woodpecker is also out of all relation to its size—a loud, vigorous, repetitive call; its drumming, too, is as frequent and as energetic as that of the greater spotted variety. The bird is especially vociferous during courtship.

Many delightful nicknames have been given to this cheerful bird, among them *Little French Woodpecker*, *Little Woodpie* and *Hickwall*.

46

The wryneck

(Iynx torquilla L.)

The wryneck is a summer visitor, arriving in late March and leaving for tropical Africa and Asia in September. Because it reaches Britain a few days before the cuckoo it is sometimes called the *Cuckoo's Mate*. It breeds fairly freely in the southern and south-eastern counties, but for some unexplained reason, its numbers appear to be decreasing steadily. The wryneck is a shy and inconspicuous bird, attracted to woodland in particular, but occasionally seen in gardens, orchards and country lanes; its mottled colouring blends effectively with its surroundings.

The wryneck is long and slender in build, with variegated grey, brown and buff upper parts and pale buff under parts. The throat bears clear dark brown bars, and the breast and flanks are speckled with dark brown marks. The tail is rounded, with prominent brown and white bars, and both bill and legs are brown.

The remarkable feature of this bird is its long flexible neck, from which its name is derived; this can be twisted completely back to front with apparent ease, the body remaining motionless. This characteristic has given rise to the nickname *Snake-bird*, the description being reinforced by its habit of hissing loudly at an intruder and darting out its long sticky tongue. This tongue enables it to scoop ants out of their burrows and to whip insects off leaves and branches. In these respects the habits of the wryneck are similar to those of the green woodpecker, although it prefers perching on a bough to clinging to the trunk. It is reported, too, that the wryneck can drum like a woodpecker, although the call which generally betrays its presence is a clamorous, ringing, rapidly-repeated note.

The wryneck does not bore into a tree like the woodpecker but does make a nest in any natural opening in a tree, a bank or a burrow. It will also gratefully make use of a nesting box. No nesting material is employed and the seven to ten eggs are white and elliptical in shape. One brood is common, though two are sometimes recorded in hot seasons. The birds pair for life.

The starling

(Sturnus vulgaris L.)*

The starling is such a familiar bird that it is not perhaps realised how handsome it is. Its plumage is glossy black, with subtle reflections of green and blue. The bill is yellow in spring, blackish in autumn. The mantle feathers are buff-tipped, the flanks and belly spotted white. It is not unlike the blackbird at first glance, but the tail is shorter, and the irridescent effect, particularly in the breeding season, is quite distinctive.

Birds which are resident in Britain migrate in the autumn, but are replaced by fresh hordes from the Continent, who take up winter quarters in countryside and town. Londoners and other city-dwellers are well aware of their noisy presence on public buildings and monuments; wherever they settle, there is always much vociferous argument and violent jockeying for position.

Apart from their nuisance value, they cannot be called destructive. Their feeding habits are certainly greedy, and they are quarrelsome, but they are fonder of insects and berries than cultivated fruit. In their quest for food they are energetic and assiduous, waddling about and probing the soil incessantly; nor are they above snatching scraps put out for other birds.

The starling has a wide assortment of calls, none of them strikingly musical, and creating a tremendous din when heard, as commonly, in chorus. Town dwellers rarely get a taste of the bird's powers of mimicry, but the calls of the curlew and song thrush are only a few of those attempted. It will also reproduce animal calls and certain mechanical noises.

Any opening in a tree, building or rock will serve as a nesting ground. Haystacks, chimney stacks and old woodpecker holes are also used. The nest is generally built by the unmated male bird, and perhaps as a result, is a bulky, untidy structure of straw, subsequently lined by the female with moss, wool and feathers. Five to seven eggs are laid, of a lovely greenish-blue colour.

The golden oriole

(Oriolus oriolus L.)*

This beautiful bird is a very infrequent visitor to Britain, mainly settling in the southern and eastern counties. Because of its comparative rarity, it is regarded as a game bird, and this persecution accounts for its decreasing numbers and characteristically secretive habits.

It is a shy and restless bird, seldom on the ground, but often hopping about on the upper branches of trees. In its favourite haunts of park and woodland, often close to water, the adult male bird is revealed as brilliant golden-yellow, with black wings and tail; the female and young, as usual, are paler, predominantly yellowish-green, with lighter under parts.

The song of the male golden oriole is clear and flutelike, carrying a long distance, and this note is usually the sole means of detecting the bird's whereabouts. These musical notes are sometimes interspersed with 'churring' alarm notes and soft, mewing calls. The bird usually keeps to the foliage, but sometimes flutters down to bathe and splash in a pool, returning to its perch with a bold upward sweep. Its food consists chiefly of insects, including large types such as grasshoppers, cockchafers and bees. In the autumn, it may also attack fruit trees and bushes.

The golden oriole's nest is remarkably elaborate, being hammock-shaped and set in the angle of two horizontal branches. Both male and female then weave it round the boughs on either side, of grass stalks, bark and pieces of wool, lining it inside with grass blades. The three or four eggs are white, with purplish-black spots.

There are more than thirty species of orioles distributed over Europe, Asia, Africa and Australasia. One of the more common is the black-naped oriole, similar in appearance to its golden cousin.

Other popular names for the golden oriole are *Golden Thrush*, *Witwol* and *Woodwale*. Possibly when Britain was more densely covered with woods this bird was more abundant.

The hawfinch

(Coccothraustes coccothraustes L.)

This is the largest of the British finches, about the size of a starling, but although fairly widely distributed, it is rarely seen, due, in part, to its shy, retiring nature and silent, unobtrusive activity. It is certainly a most distinctive bird, with its large head, enormous parrot-shaped beak, thick neck and short tail. Its colour is mainly brown, with black wings and a prominent white patch on the shoulder. The huge beak varies in colour according to the season. The young have a yellow throat, with spotted and barred under parts.

The hawfinch roosts in woods and heavy foliage, and can sometimes be spotted perching bolt upright on a bough. It is also, to every serious gardener's dismay, a frequent and fearless visitor to orchards and market gardens. Among its favourite articles of diet are green peas and the kernels of fruits, especially cherries and plums. The massive beak makes short work of pea-pods, ripping them lengthwise to reach the peas, whilst the horny pads inside the beak are used for collecting fruit stones, which are then split open. Berries of holly and yew are also eaten, and the presence of empty pods, split fruit stones and pecked berries, are sure signs of the bird's recent activities. Various popular names such as *Grosbeak*, *Cherry Finch* and *Berry Breaker* reflect these unmistakable features and tendencies.

The nest is a shallow affair of twigs, lined with hair and fibre, and built on the horizontal branch of a tree, or in a bush. Four to six eggs are laid, greyish-green, with black and brown streaks and spots. Like the bird itself, the nest and eggs are rarely seen. The young hawfinches are fed mainly on insects and caterpillars, and this partly offsets the destructive practises of the bird. The fledglings are born with the menacing beak, which will shortly reap such havoc.

The hawfinch is unusual among finches in that there is no closely related species.

The greenfinch

(Chloris chloris L.)

Similarly built to the hawfinch, but far more sociable and infinitely less destructive, is the greenfinch. It also has a powerful, parrot-like bill, but its main diet consists of seeds, grain, berries and small insects. The male bird is handsomely garbed, its plumage being mainly olive-green, the wings merging from grey to brown, with bright yellow patches. The base of the tail is likewise yellow, and the cleft tail is conspicuous in flight.

The greenfinch is not much seen in gardens, but congregates in large flocks in fields and along hedgerows, often in the company of chaffinches, linnets and blue tits. Its song is not particularly melodious, in fact little more than a monotonous, discordant cry, repeated with little variation for hours on end. It is one of the few birds which sing while actually flying, especially during courtship.

At this time, the male greenfinch puts on a truly remarkable aerial display for the benefit of his mate, fluttering and circling like a bat, twittering incessantly. Indeed, at all times the male is most attentive to the female, feeding her with regurgitated pulp both before and during incubation.

The nest is a large, untidy structure of twigs, moss, grass and feathers, built in a hedge, bush or evergreen. The four to six eggs vary enormously in colour, but are usually greenish-blue to dull white, with occasional spots and streaks of purple at one end. Two or three broods are raised, the young birds being fed by both parents by regurgitation, and the mother is exceptionally devoted to them. It is not unknown for the female greenfinch to erect an elementary awning of leaves, in order to protect her nest from the sun.

The greenfinch, like most of its family, is a resident bird, and no extensive migration is recorded. Large flocks do, however, visit Britain during the winter.

Among the many nicknames of this bird are *Green Grosbeak, Green Linnet* and *Bighead.*

The serin

(Serinus canarius L.)

The serin, or serin finch, is closely related to the wild canary found in the Canary Islands and the Azores, and to the better-known domestic canary. It is a rare visitor to Britain, although breeding freely in central and southern Europe. It is a small bird, the upper parts being olive-green, streaked grey-brown, the under parts yellow, streaked with grey and brown on the flanks. The female is additionally streaked on throat and breast.

It is a bird of field, garden and hedgerow, nesting in bushes and trees. The nest is made of plant stems and roots, decorated with lichen and lined with hair. The three to five eggs are pale blue or grey, with reddish-brown spots.

The serin is an insect and seed eater, and like its canary relatives, it has a pleasant, twittering song.

The linnet

(Carduelis cannabina L.)

The linnet is one of the more common British finches and very gregarious. Its plumage alters considerably from season to season, and it is known variously as the *Red, Brown* and *Grey Linnet*. The male is seen at his best in the spring, when in addition to a reddish-brown mantle and pale white under parts, he boasts a crimson head and breast.

Among the linnet's favourite haunts are gardens, hedgerows, heaths and marshes. Its nest is often found in bramble and thorn thickets only a few feet from the ground. It is made of grass, roots and moss and is lined with hair, down and feathers. There are four to six eggs, bluish-white or grey, with red and purple blotches. Food consists chiefly of weed seeds and insects, with oats and berries in winter.

The goldfinch

(Carduelis carduelis L.*)*

The goldfinch is one of the smallest and daintiest of all finches, and was, until protected by law, a popular cage bird. Its colouring is vivid—a pattern of crimson, black and white on head and throat, tawny under parts, black wings slashed with a broad gold bar, and a black tail tipped with white. The hen is similar in colour to the cock.

It is seen during breeding time in gardens, orchards and on cultivated land. In trees it seems to prefer the highest and outermost branches, rather than the foliage. In winter, flocks descend along the road-sides and on weed-infested wasteland. It feeds on seeds of all kinds, particularly thistles, chickweed, groundsel and dandelions, and since it also likes insects, farmers regard it as a staunch friend.

Its fluttering flight is dainty and graceful, like all its movements, somewhat like that of a butterfly, and whilst flying it twitters continuously and melodiously. The song is similar to that of the canary. Sometimes it will perch on a seed-head, clinging to it like a tit. During courtship, the male puts on an extravagant and varied display, spreading his wings, exhibiting his plumage, and swaying his body from side to side.

The goldfinch's nest is neatly and laboriously constructed, generally in a bush, or in a chestnut or fruit tree. It is roomy, cup-shaped, made of dry grass, fine roots and moss, and lined with thistledown. It is a little like the chaffinch's, but on a smaller scale. Four or five eggs are laid, bluish-white, with purplish-brown spots and streaks. The young, which are called 'Greypates', are fed on regurgitated food. They have brownish heads and their backs are streaked brown. They also have the distinctive black and gold-banded wings, but lack the parents' gay head pattern.

Among the many colourful names for the goldfinch are *Sweet William, Goldie, Red Linnet* and *King Harry.*

The British species is commonest in the southern counties, and local migrations occur in autumn and winter.

The bullfinch

(Pyrrhula pyrrhula L.)*

This beautiful bird is secretive in habit, but fairly widely distributed throughout the British Isles. It prefers the dense foliage of woods and hedgerows, but during the spring pays rather unwelcome visits to gardens and orchards.

It is a plump bird, with a thick, rounded black beak. The under parts are salmon-red in the male, pinkish-grey in the female. The white rump is distinctive to both sexes. The adult male has a black head, grey back, blue-black tail and wings, the latter tinged with white. The female is duller, and the young resemble her, but have no black cap.

The bullfinch is a shy bird and is rarely seen far from cover. It is not a great singer, but its low warble is usually delivered sitting bolt upright, inflating the chest and swaying the head sideways. Like all finches, it is fond of bathing, and can sometimes be observed splashing in a pool, and sipping from the clear water.

Its most unpopular habit is the indiscriminate attacking and ripping off of fruit buds in the spring, which has earned it such names as *Plum-bird, Bud-bird* and *Bud-picker*. It destroys far more than it can possibly eat, leaving quantities of buds at the base of trees and bushes. Buds of flowering plants are similarly attacked, but it redeems itself to the extent of dining mainly on insects later in the summer.

The bullfinch breeds in hedges, shrubberies and brambles, the nest being placed about six feet above ground level. It seems barely large enough to admit such a plump bird, and is made of twigs, interlaced with thick black roots. The four or five eggs are greenish-blue, with a few purplish-brown specks and streaks. Two broods are common, the first eggs being laid late in April.

It is one of the few British birds which pairs for life, and unlike most finches, it does not flock when cold weather arrives. An allied species, the northern bullfinch, larger and even more brightly coloured, joins it occasionally during the winter.

The chaffinch

(Fringilla coelebs L.)*

Commonest of all native finches is the chaffinch, a popular, easily-tamed bird, bright of hue and a welcome garden visitor. For Robert Browning, in Italy, it had nostalgic associations:

'. . . While the chaffinch sings on the orchard bough,

In England—now!'

Certainly it is a loud and cheerful singer, especially in spring, the joyful melody descending in tone and finishing in a challenging flourish. Its nature echoes its song, being most sociable, as it flits among the thickets and hedgerows, and joins sparrows and greenfinches on arable land, less conveniently, after the wheat sowing.

The adult male is particularly handsome, with his blue nape and crown, body of varying shades of brown, rump yellowish-green, wings and tail blue-black streaked with white. Both the female and young are paler and more evenly brown, but both sexes have a recognisable white shoulder patch. The chaffinch feeds mainly on weed seeds, fruit seeds and grain, but insects are also freely taken and fed to the fledglings. The bird will also gratefully accept scraps put out in winter.

The chaffinch builds its nest in small trees, bushes and hedges, fairly close to the ground. It is extremely carefully and compactly made of moss, fine grasses and hairs, intricately woven together, and decorated on the outside with lichen. When completed, it is often difficult to detect among the surrounding foliage. The hen does the actual building, while the cock helps to collect the building material, and lends her strong vocal encouragement. Four to six eggs are laid, two or three times in a season, and varying in colour from greenish-blue to grey, generally with dark brown markings.

Another finch closely resembling the chaffinch is the brambling, which arrives in Britain for the winter from the colder regions of Scandinavia. Its call, and its nest and eggs, are all similar to those of the chaffinch.

The yellowhammer

(Emberiza citrinella L.)

The yellowhammer is a member of the bunting family, and the 'hammer' part of the name is actually derived from the German word for bunting. It is a very common bird, generally distributed throughout Britain, larger and bolder than the similar but rarer species of cirl bunting. It has a bright yellow head and throat, yellow and brown mottled breast, yellow under parts, chestnut wings and tail, with white outer tail feathers, clearly visible in flight. The female is duller in hue, and the young do not acquire any yellow until after the first moult.

It is a cheerful, sociable bird, frequently seen perching on hedgerows and telegraph poles, and in the winter flitting round haystacks and among the stubble, in the company of finches and sparrows. It sings throughout the spring and summer, very often in the full heat of day. Its familiar and characteristic song has been likened to the jingle, 'Little bit of bread and no cheese,' the final note being at a different pitch and longer sustained than the rest. One of its nicknames, in fact, is *Bread and Cheese*.

The yellow bunting, as it is also called, eats all kinds of vegetable matter, corn, weed seeds, berries, and also insects. Almost all its food is found at ground level, and its nest, too, is generally built either on or near the ground, in the bottom of hedges or in gorse thickets. The nest is composed of grass, fibre and hair. The breeding period is prolonged, sometimes from May to September, during which time two or three broods may be reared. Three to five eggs are laid, greyish or purplish-white, with a few spots or irregular brown lines. These pencil-like markings have given rise to other popular names, such as *Scribbling* or *Writing Lark*.

Besides the cirl bunting, other members of the family include the corn bunting, pine bunting, black-headed and red-headed buntings, ortolan bunting, reed bunting and others. They are, on the whole, more delicately built than the finches.

The skylark

(Alauda arvensis L.)*

The skylark is one of the most renowned and popular of all birds, and its praises have been sung by poets throughout the ages. In apparent contradiction, one of its local names is *Groundlark,* but this is accurate since the bird spends much of its time on the ground, rarely settling on trees. It can walk and run, but never hops; when uneasy, it crouches low. Its diet consists of weed seeds, corn and small insects. In appearance it is fairly undistinguished, a blend of light and dark brown, with prominent white outer tail feathers, visible in flight. It also has a distinctive crest, which can be erected at will.

The song of the male skylark in flight is, of course, its chief glory and claim to fame. It consists of a vehement and unbroken succession of trills, and the higher the bird flies, the more lovely does this lyrical warbling seem to sound. Shelley's beautiful poem is too well-known to quote, and so are Shakespeare's rapturous greetings to the lark singing at heaven's gate. George Meredith accurately and lovingly described the song as a 'silver chain of many links without a break.' Whilst singing, the lark soars to tremendous heights, almost vertically, then drifts in wide circles, head to wind, descending in spirals, silent once more as it alights.

Being terrestrial in habit, the skylark builds its nest, made of grasses, on the ground, in any suitable depression. In harvest time, the nest is frequently disturbed or destroyed, and the attentive parents have to carry their young, in their claws, to a safer home. Three or four eggs are laid, greyish-white, sometimes tinged with green and speckled thickly with dark brown markings.

Very similar to the skylark is the woodlark, though smaller and with a shorter tail. Its nesting habits and diet are similar to the skylark's, and if it does not climb to the same dizzy heights, its song is thought by many to be even more melodious, though with more interruptions. It has also been known to sing at night.

The tree pipit

(Anthus trivialis L.)

A widely distributed summer visitor to Britain, remaining from April to September, the tree pipit is closely related to the wagtail family. In fact, however, it more closely resembles the larks, and among its more familiar local names are *Singing Titlark, Tree Lark, Field Lark* and *Meadow Lark.* It is commonly seen on the fringes of woods, in parks and open glades, on heaths and on railway embankments. Though rarely venturing far from cover, it is not attracted to dense woodland.

The adult male tree pipit has light brown upper parts and buff under parts, freely streaked all over with dark brown marks, except for the rump. The belly is dull white, and the tail feathers have white tips. A dark moustachial stripe borders the throat; the legs and toes are flesh-coloured. After autumn the general colouring is buffer and richer. The bird is rather smaller than the related meadow pipit and may be distinguished by its shorter and more curved hind claw.

The tree pipit is an unostentatious bird and rarely embarks on long flights. Like the meadow pipit it has a curious shuttlecock flight, rising from the topmost branches of a tree, hovering for a while about twenty feet above it, then dropping down, often to the same branch, with fully spread wings and tail. During this excursion it trills away loudly and cheerfully, usually ending its song with three emphatic, melodious notes. It also has a distinctive alarm note.

Untrue to its name, the tree pipit nests on the ground, well concealed under bracken or in long grass. The nest is built of grass, moss and roots, lined with finer roots and hair, sometimes with a tiny entrance. Four to six eggs are laid and these are extraordinarily varied in colour, generally with a greyish-white or reddish-brown ground, and densely speckled and blotched with red, brown and purple. One or two broods are raised. Both the tree pipit and meadow pipit are much victimised by the cuckoo.

The yellow wagtail

(Motacilla flava L.*)*

The yellow wagtail is a summer visitor to Britain, a bird of dainty and neat appearance, possibly the loveliest and most graceful of its family. The upper parts are olive-green, the under parts clear yellow. There is a bright yellow streak above the eye and ear covert. Wings and tail are brownish-black, with buff edges to the feathers, the outer tail feathers being white. The female, and the male outside the breeding season, is duller, being browner above and paler beneath.

The yellow wagtail is a great lover of water, and generally settles in meadows, pastureland and marshes. Like other members of the family, it both walks and runs, head constantly bobbing, tail flicking restlessly up and down. The tail is also a prominent feature of the male bird's courting posture, being spread out like a fan. During this display the male will often break out into brief song, but the bird is generally silent.

The wagtail's food consists mainly of insects and their larvae, and small snails. The bird may often be seen in freshly ploughed fields, or flitting among cattle. In some parts it is known as *Cow-bird*, in others as *Yellow Molly* and *Quaketail*.

Meadows and cornfields are among the favourite nesting places, and any slight depression in the ground, a hoof-print or wheel-track, for example, will serve. The nest is constructed of dry grass and roots, lined with hair, feathers and wool. The eggs are four to six in number, greyish-white and thickly mottled with reddish-brown marks. The cuckoo is often an unwelcome caller to the nest.

There are numerous other wagtails, notably the pied wagtail, one of the commonest native species, black and white, and also one of the cuckoo's favourite victims; it, too, is very partial to water and is known as *Water Wagtail*, or, more amusingly, *Dishwasher*. Then there are the blue-headed and grey-headed wagtails, both rare summer visitors, and the white wagtail, similar to the pied in habits and appearance.

72

The grey wagtail

(Motacilla cinerea Tunst.)

The grey wagtail, sometimes called winter wagtail, is one of the less common resident British birds and is also a summer migrant, wintering in Africa. It is most often found in hilly districts and almost always near running water. Swift-running streams are particularly favoured, but the bird is sometimes seen on the banks of lakes and rivers. It tends to desert the highlands at the approach of winter, moving southwards and even reaching coastal districts.

Its name is misleading, for its plumage is a blend of yellow, grey and white. Like the yellow wagtail it has a sulphur-yellow breast and under parts, but the upper parts are slate-grey, the rump greenish-yellow, the wings dusky brown, the tail brown edged with white; the tail is longer than that of the related pied wagtail, though the body is slightly shorter. In breeding time the male's grey head is streaked with white above the eye, and the throat is black; in winter the throat is white. During the elaborate courtship display all these handsome colours are revealed at their finest.

Like other members of the family the grey wagtail may be identified by its dainty tripping gait, head and tail dipping with every step. It walks or runs along the side of the stream or perches on a convenient branch, on the alert for water insects. Sometimes it will conduct its search in the stream itself, stepping from stone to stone, the water rippling over its feet. Its diet is made up of insects and small crustaceans.

The flight of the grey wagtail is typically undulating and the tail is raised and spread on landing. It is not a gifted songster but its brief twittering is rather like that of the pied wagtail.

The nest is built close to the water, usually in a hole in a wall or crevice in a rock. It is constructed of grass and roots and lined with hair. Four to six eggs are laid, buff with faint grey-brown hairlines, and they are often indistinguishable from those of the yellow and pied wagtails. Two broods are usually reared.

The nuthatch

(Sitta europaea L.*)*

Although sometimes called *Blue Woodpecker*, the nuthatch has little in common with the woodpecker tribe, apart from its pointed bill and tree-climbing ability. In the latter respect, it is far more agile and acrobatic, more so even than the tree creeper. Using only its strong, curved claws, and unsupported by its tail, it clambers up and down, and from side to side of tree trunks with complete ease. It can equally well hang upside down from a bough, and, like the nightjar, commonly perches lengthwise along it. Some think it even sleeps upside down.

The nuthatch is a short, plump bird, its upper parts blue-grey, serving as effective camouflage among the trees, its under parts buff, its flanks chestnut. A distinctive black band crosses the eye region, and the throat is white. The central tail feathers are grey, the others black with white and grey tips. The nuthatch's dipping, deliberate flight from tree to tree is unmistakable, but the bird is hard to detect either at rest or in the air.

The name is derived from the bird's habit of wedging a nut in a crack of the bark, and hammering it with the full weight of its powerful body until the kernel is extracted. A less ambiguous name, therefore, and often employed, is the *Nuthack*. Hazel nuts are its favourite, but acorns, yew seeds and insects are commonly eaten. Quite often, nuts will be stored, squirrel-like, for later use.

Its nesting habits are also ingenious, a hole in a tree, perhaps an old woodpecker's nest, being sufficient. Enlarging the hole, where necessary, presents no problems, but often the entrance has to be narrowed in order to keep away intruders. The nuthatch will accomplish this by plastering the entrance with mud or clay, until it is just wide enough to admit the parent bird. With both parents and their brood in the nest together, there is not much breathing space. Wood chips, bark and dead leaves serve as a lining to the nest, and five to eight eggs are laid, white in colour, speckled light red.

The great tit

(Parus major L.*)*

Largest of the tit or titmouse family, the great tit is an aggressive and valiant bird. It is common to all parts of Britain, and is most gregarious. It is a plump, short-billed bird, its head, chin and throat being black, with a distinctive black band down the centre of its yellow breast. The upper parts are yellowish-green, rump, wings and tail blue-grey, with a white bar on the wings and white tips to the tail.

The great tit is a voracious eater, and has an unpleasant habit of attacking small birds and certain types of bees; this has earned it the name of *Bee-biter* in some districts. It also destroys buds, peas and ripe fruit. These propensities are, however, outweighed by its colossal appetite for harmful insects and caterpillars. It has been reckoned that a pair of great tits can kill over seven thousand insects, mainly caterpillars, in about three weeks. Berries, nuts, fat, bones and kitchen scraps are equally welcome, as is the familiar coconut, especially in winter.

Like all its relatives, the great tit is sprightly and acrobatic in its movements, and will hang in every conceivable position, including head downwards, in its unceasing search for food. It has a tremendous repertory of calls, prominent among which are a series of rasping, metallic notes, which has led to another nickname, *Saw-sharpener*.

The great tit is adaptable where nesting places are concerned, practically any opening anywhere sufficing. Trees, walls, posts, burrows, discarded nests, bee-hives, nesting boxes, shelves, letter-boxes, flower-pots—it is not particular. Both sexes build the nest of moss, grass and feathers, and six to nine or more eggs are laid, white, speckled reddish-brown. The mother is quick to defend her nest, and like the blue tit, hisses at intruders.

Other members of the family are the coal tit, smaller and duller in plumage, the marsh tit and willow tit, both woodland birds, and the blue, crested and long-tailed tits.

The blue tit

(Parus coeruleus L.)*

The blue tit, or tomtit, is smaller than the great tit, and can readily be distinguished by its light blue crown, wings and tail, the crown having a white border. Nape and cheeks are white, with a blue band passing through the eye and joining a dark blue collar band. The upper parts are green, the under parts yellow. The blue wings are also barred with white.

In habit the blue tit much resembles the great tit, although the two birds have a rooted dislike for each other and will frequently fight. The blue tit has the friendlier nature and its antics are even more acrobatic. It sometimes hops about on trees like a tree creeper and will build a nest in any available opening. Seven to ten or more eggs are laid, white, speckled light reddish-brown.

The blue tit is also a tremendous devourer of noxious insects, though attacking fruit buds and ripe fruit as well.

The crested tit

(Parus cristatus L.)*

This is one of the smaller members of the titmouse family, which makes its home in the pine woods of Scotland, and is rarely seen in other parts of Britain. Its distinguishing feature is the black and white head crest. The sides of the head are white, with a semi-circular black band around the eye region. Another black patch extends to the base of the crest and over the throat. The upper parts, wings and tail are pale brown, the under parts white, tinged with brown.

The Scottish crested tit breeds generally in old stumps of pine, its nest being made of moss, and lined generously with hairs and feathers. The five or six eggs are white, heavily blotched reddish-brown.

The coal tit

(Parus ater L.)

This sprightly member of the titmouse family is widely distributed throughout Britain, but is not as common as the great tit or blue tit. It inhabits all types of woodland, especially fir plantations, and spends more time than they do among trees. Its feeding habits are similar to theirs—insects, nuts, berries, seeds and kitchen scraps.

The coal tit has a blue-black head, neck and throat, white cheeks and a distinctive white patch on the nape of the neck. The upper parts are olive brown, the under parts white shading to buff. The wings show a double white bar, the bill is black, the legs and toes grey. Both sexes are alike, and the young lack the adult sheen on the head.

Like all tits it is highly acrobatic and hops on tree trunks like the tree creeper. The nest is built in a hole, a tree stump, a rabbit burrow, a squirrel drey or a nesting box. It is similar to the great tit's, a thick pad of hair and grass with a mossy foundation. Seven to ten eggs are laid, white, thickly speckled reddish-brown.

The willow tit

(Parus atricapillus L.)

This is a very rare bird, only recognised about sixty years ago as a separate species. In appearance it is similar to the almost equally uncommon marsh tit, except that its head is brownish-black whereas the marsh tit's is glossy blue-black. Both birds keep well away from human habitation. The willow tit is a bird of the hedgerows, copses and woods, and feeds on insects, seeds and nuts.

The upper parts are olive-brown, the under parts buff, the wings and tail brown. A buff patch on the secondary wing feathers is noticeable when the bird is hanging upside down and the tail is rounder at the end than that of the marsh tit.

The willow tit generally nests in a rotten tree stump, birch, willow and alder being favoured. It often excavates its own hole and carries the chips a little distance away before discarding them. The nest itself is a shallow cup of felted hair, fur, wood chips and occasional feathers. Five to nine eggs are common, white with reddish-brown spots.

The long-tailed tit

(Aegithalos caudatus **L.***)*

Easily recognisable by its small pink, white and black body, and long, rudder-like tail, this attractive bird is a tree lover, feeding almost wholly on insects. Its nest is most unusually and beautifully constructed either in a bush or bramble, or in the fork of a tree. It is oval in shape, built by both male and female from the inside, and woven of moss, cobweb and hair. It is covered with lichen and lined with a vast quantity of feathers, more than two thousand actually having been found in a single nest. It is hardly surprising that the nest takes two or three weeks to complete.

The entrance to the nest is a minute hole high up on one side. The number of eggs varies from six to twenty, white, and marked in different ways. The tits are devoted parents, and there is strong family loyalty, even after the young have left the nest.

The goldcrest

(Regulus regulus **L.***)*

This bird, about three and a half inches long, is the smallest of all European birds. It is widely distributed, preferring coniferous forests, but is not easy to spot, since it rarely settles on the ground. The plumage is mainly olive-green above and dull white below. The name is derived from the bright yellow, black-bordered crests of both sexes, the male having an orange patch in the centre.

The nest is most intricately made, slung from the branch of a fir tree, woven of moss and spiders' webs, and lined with feathers. The eggs, seven to twelve of them, are no larger than peas, and are covered with faint, reddish-brown speckles. The goldcrest is a devourer of harmful insects, including greenfly, and is as accomplished an acrobat as the tits, with whom it may be seen during the winter.

84

The red-backed shrike

(Lanius collurio L.)

A summer visitor, and the only member of the shrike family to nest in Britain, the red-backed shrike is a compact, predatory bird, known, by reason of its more cruel and unpleasant habits, as the *Butcher Bird*. It is handsome to look at, its back being chestnut-brown rather than a literal red, its nape and crown grey, with a black band across the forehead and through the eyes; the rump is grey, the under parts buff, and the tail black, with white outer feathers. The bill is hooked and toothed, and both the long tail and pointed wings are clearly recognisable in flight.

The red-backed shrike considers most similar-sized animals and birds as its legitimate prey. It perches silently on a tree, fence or telegraph wire, and from such a vantage-point swoops directly on its prey in hawk-like fashion. Among its victims are rabbits, hedgehogs, voles, field-mice, shrews, frogs, lizards, bees, spiders, worms and young birds. The shrike then carries its prey back to the perch, where, if sufficiently large, it is methodically dismembered. Alternatively, it will impale an animal or bird on a sharp thorn, leaving the body in this gruesome larder for future reference.

The shrike's nest is generally found in bushes, hedgerows or brambles. It is built by the male bird, and is a large, rather untidy structure of grass and moss, lined with roots and hairs. Five to six eggs are laid, very variable in colour, white, grey, green and pink, freely spotted.

Two other well-known members of this carnivorous family are the woodchat and great grey shrikes, both occasional visitors to the British Isles, especially in the autumn and winter, in the east and south-east. The woodchat shrike has black and white plumage and a bright brown crown. The grey shrike is a fairly large bird, with grey upper parts, white beneath, with black and white wings and tail. Both are drawn towards wooded districts, and have similar feeding habits to their red-backed relative.

The willow warbler

(Phylloscopus trochilus L.*)*

This tiny bird, also called the *Willow Wren*, is one of the most welcome spring and summer visitors to Britain, and in midsummer the woods resound to its sweet, rippling song. This consists of ascending and descending scales of successive short notes, gathering in volume, then dying away to silence. It is a graceful, restless bird as it flits about the foliage —olive-green and yellow above, white and yellow beneath. It feeds exclusively on insects, and builds a neat dome-shaped nest of moss and dry grass, lined with feathers, with a side entrance. It is usually found low down, either on the ground, or in the bottom of a hedge or bush. The six to eight eggs are white, speckled and streaked brown and red.

Among the commonest nicknames of this endearing bird are *Tom Thumb, Miller's Thumb* and *Haybird.*

The chiffchaff

(Phylloscopus collybita Vieill.*)*

The chiffchaff, closely related to the willow warbler, is also a summer guest from the Mediterranean, but arrives even earlier. Its song, a simple 'chiff-chaff', repeated over and over again, can be heard from the middle of March onwards. It is smaller than the willow warbler, and has a more rounded wing. It is also rather plainer in overall colour. The chiffchaff flies about the treetops and nests fairly high up. The nest is bulky, of leaves, grass and moss, also dome-shaped and feather-lined, with a side entrance. The eggs are similar to the willow warbler's.

The chiffchaff is a cheerful, sociable bird, singing all summer and living in harmony with its warbler cousin. It feeds entirely on insects. Besides the names mentioned above, it is also sometimes called *Chip-chop* and *Thummie.*

The reed warbler

(Acrocephalus scirpaceus Herm.*)*

Another April to September resident in Britain, the reed warbler, as its name implies, is most at home in marshland, in wet ditches and along the banks of slow-flowing streams and rivers. It is not a particularly distinguished-looking bird, with dark brown upper parts, rufous towards the rump, buff flanks and under parts, white throat and belly, and greyish-brown wings and tail. Both sexes are alike in appearance.

The reed warbler is rarely seen at any distance from water, and its flight is short and jerky. Most of the time it hops and creeps among the reeds in search of its staple diet of aquatic insects, which include dragonflies and mayflies. In late summer, certain berries and fruits are also eaten. At times it will perch on a swaying reed to sing, and its rather monotonous, crooning melody can be heard at all times of day, especially towards dusk, and even, like that of others of the warbler family, at night. Were it not for this continuous chattering, the bird would often be overlooked, for its inconspicuous brown body is generally well concealed among the reeds.

The reed warbler's nest is cylindrical and generally deep. It is usually built near the water, but is occasionally found in lilac or wild rose bushes. Some have even been discovered in willow trees. The nest is wonderfully made of grass, strips of reed and water weeds, lined with grass and reed flowers. Very often the nest is woven round and supported by two or three reed stems. The whole structure protects both eggs and young even when the wind is buffeting and swaying the reeds outside. Four or five eggs are laid, greenish-white, speckled olive and grey. They are frequently disturbed by the cuckoo.

Another member of the family is the sedge warbler, which is a more common bird and more distinctive, with brown plumage and a white streak over the eye. The grasshopper warbler is less often seen, because of its secretive nature. It flutters about the undergrowth, betraying its presence only by its peculiar song, a continuous, high, whirring grasshopper-like note, rising and falling in tone.

The marsh warbler

(Acrocephalus palustris Bech.)

The marsh warbler is one of the rarest of British breeding birds and is generally confined to a few southern counties. It spends the winter in Africa, often as far south as the Cape, and is a late migrant, not usually making an appearance until early June. In shape and colouring it is practically indistinguishable from the related reed warbler, except that the upper parts are rather more olive, the under parts a brighter yellow and the rump a little duller; the wings are very slightly longer.

The song of the marsh warbler, however, is richer and more varied, at times almost as melodious as that of the blackcap. It may be heard clearly by day and by night, usually emerging from a tree top; it is, however, of fairly short duration, coming to an end during July. Since the bird's habits are shy and skulking, the song is often the only guide to its presence. In addition, the marsh warbler is a skilful mimic, and among the calls imitated are those of the nightingale and the jackdaw.

The bird may be found alongside lakes and rivers, on marshland, among reed or willow beds, in ditches or on waste ground overgrown with weeds. Its flight is short and jerky, and like the reed warbler it creeps furtively amidst the water vegetation, feeding on aquatic insects and occasionally on berries. The nest itself is never placed directly over water and is not always found in marshes; it is sometimes built in a bush or even in a cornfield. Cup-shaped, but shallower than the reed warbler's, it is made of grass, hair and moss, sometimes lined with a few roots. It is generally suspended from the stems of marsh plants—meadow-sweet being especially popular—by means of 'basket-handles', loops of nesting material encircling the cup. In the nest are laid four or five eggs, with a bluish or greenish ground colour, sparsely but boldly speckled olive-brown, dark brown or violet. The eggs are laid in mid-June, and one brood is reared.

The lesser whitethroat

(Sylvia curruca L.)*

The lesser whitethroat is a smaller and greyer bird than the common whitethroat, with more markedly arboreal habits. It spends the winter in northern Africa and arrives in Britain during late April or early May. Its predominant colours are grey and white. The adult male in spring has brownish-grey upper parts and whitish under parts; chin and throat are white, wings brown with pale margins, tail brown with white-tipped outer feathers, bill and legs grey. The female is similar but paler, the young somewhat browner.

Although generally well-concealed in a thick hedgerow, bramble or shrub, the lesser whitethroat often reveals its presence by its song, a loud metallic rattle, rather like that of the cirl bunting. It also produces a low, musical warble which tails off into the familiar rattle, but this song can only be heard very close at hand. The bird sometimes sings during its brief flights from one hedgerow to another, and continues during the hottest weather. Unlike the common whitethroat, it does not indulge in 'sky-rocketing' antics, and is, on the whole, a far quieter and more inconspicuous bird. Its food consists mainly of insects, sometimes captured on the wing, and soft fruit, especially currants.

The lesser whitethroat builds its nest in any kind of hedge, bush, shrub or thicket, generally a few feet from the ground and at a higher level than that of the common whitethroat. It is also much smaller and frailer in structure, being built of grass, hair and small roots and lined with fibre and other local materials. Occasionally the nest is suspended in the manner of the reed or marsh warbler's. Four to six eggs are laid, creamy white, boldly marked with brown blotches and lighter grey and violet patches. One brood is common, and both parents share the incubation. They attend the eggs closely and if disturbed will move a short distance away, returning as soon as the danger is past.

The common whitethroat

(Sylvia communis L.)

This bird is the most common of all warblers, though like the others it deserts Britain in the autumn for warmer countries. Its favourite haunts are in wasteland or common, or any district with scrub growth. The adult male has an ash-grey head and neck, with a slight crest, raised when singing, and a pure white throat. The upper parts are reddish-brown, under parts pinkish-white. The wings are brown, edged with red, the tail also brown, with white outer feathers. The female has a brown head.

Not as secretive as most warblers, the common whitethroat is constantly on the move, particularly active among the hedgerows and undergrowth. Scuttling around among nettles and other weeds has earned it the nickname of *Nettle-creeper*. Its food consists chiefly of insects, and later of small berries and soft fruits; raspberries and currants are especially popular.

It is not built for flying long distances, but can be recognised by the curious jerking and darting fashion in which it launches itself from hedge to hedge, singing as it goes. The song itself is a mixture of pleasant warbling notes and harsh, grating sounds, abruptly cut short, and can be heard throughout the summer, apart from a brief period during July when moulting takes place. The whitethroat's carefree aerial dancing display has gained it another perceptive local name, *Singing Skyrocket*.

The whitethroat builds its nest close to the ground, in hedges, in brambles or among nettles, the male commencing the work with grass and roots before the arrival of the hen, who lines and decorates it with down, hair and wool. The four or five eggs are very variable in colour, ranging from greenish-white to yellow or buff, and speckled with pale brown. Should the nest be threatened during incubation, the parent birds will flutter round, uttering sharp warning cries; and if the nest is approached whilst the fledglings are in it, the adult may shuffle about close to the nest, feigning lameness.

The blackcap

(Sylvia atricapilla L.)

One of the most popular summer migrants, and justifiably so, is the blackcap, or *Nightingale of the North*, as it is often called. The adult male has a glossy black crown (reddish-brown in the female and young), upper parts greyish-brown, sides of head, neck and under parts pale grey (brown in female), merging into off-white. It is commonly seen in open woodland, along hedgerows and in gardens.

The blackcap's distinguishing feature is its delightful and melodious song, being short, rich, perfectly phrased and modulated, similar to the equally musical song of the garden warbler, but even more varied. Remarkable, too, is the ability to imitate the songs and call-notes of more than a dozen other local birds, and to incorporate them in its own repertory, the nightingale's being one. The song can be heard for a distance of over one hundred yards, and is particularly lovely early in the season. During the courting period the bird puts on a dress display, raising the head feathers, puffing out the body feathers, drooping the wings, and vigorously agitating the tail.

The blackcap's diet consists of insects early in the season, and later of berries, peas, and a variety of fruits, including cherries, strawberries, raspberries and currants. It will sometimes strip an elder bush of its fruit.

Its usual breeding grounds are bushes, hedgerows and brambles, often among honeysuckle and wild roses. The male bird helps to build the nest, which is made of dried grass, and lined with finer grass and hairs. Both the nest and the four to six eggs, cream or yellow speckled and clouded brown, are like those of the garden warbler; the male also helps to incubate the eggs.

Sometimes the nests of the two species can be found in the same bush, though as a rule, the birds shun each other's company. If the blackcap's young are threatened, the parent birds may feign injury, a practice common to many smaller birds who lack other obvious means of defence.

The garden warbler

(Sylvia borin Bodd.)

The description is misleading because the garden warbler is essentially a woodland bird. It is a summer visitor, wintering in central and south Africa, and usually arrives late in May. Its favourite haunts are on the fringes or in a clearing of a wood, on heaths and commons, in osier beds and in copses. Occasionally it will venture into gardens in search of fruit.

Like other gifted song birds, the garden warbler is undistinguished in appearance and retiring in habits; it is therefore seen infrequently. The upper parts are olive-brown, the under parts buffish-white. Throat, breast and flanks are buff, the cheeks are grey, and there is a faint pale streak over the eye. The bird's chief claim to recognition is its song, a glorious and melodious warble, not very different from that of the blackcap, but rather lower in tone and more sustained. When the two birds are singing together, as they sometimes do even from the same thicket or shrub, it is very difficult to tell them apart. Although one of the most musical of birds, the familiar and local names given to it, such as *Garden Whitethroat, Haychat* and *Fauvette*, hardly pay tribute to its vocal powers.

Insects form the bird's main nourishment, flies being caught on the wing, but berries and soft fruis are also popular. Its flight is rapid and jerky. The nest is generally placed fairly low down in a bush, an evergreen shrub or a bramble, further down than the blackcap's. Both sexes help to build, and may tackle two or three before they are completely satisfied with their work. The finished nest is frail but roomy, made of twisted dried grass and lined with hair and fine roots. Both birds also help to incubate the eggs, which, like the blackcap's, are variable in colour, usually white or greenish-white and speckled or blotched with brown. If the nest is approached or disturbed, the sitting bird will slip away, reappearing immediately the intruder has gone. Two broods are sometimes raised.

The song thrush

(Turdus ericetorum Turt.*)*

A general favourite is the song thrush, or throstle, not because of any marked sociability, but for its vigorous song, which continues all the year round, even after dusk. The bird can be seen in woodland, in hedgerows, and in shrubberies and gardens. It has a strong preference for inhabited districts. Some resident birds migrate in the autumn, but continental varieties replace them.

Like many songsters, it is not remarkable for its colouring; upper parts are olive-brown, under parts creamy-white, with blackish-brown spots. The female is smaller and paler beneath.

The song thrush can often be seen hopping about, head cocked, searching for worms, slugs and snails; the last are smashed open against boulders or walls. It is also fond of soft fruit and berries, but does not cause tremendous damage in the garden.

The song, delivered as a rule from cover, is loud and clear, made up of simple phrases, generally repeated. Browning, in his *Home Thoughts from Abroad*, noted this peculiarity:

'That's the wise thrush; he sings each song twice over,
Lest you should think he never could recapture
The first fine careless rapture!'

The thrush also has great powers of mimicry, and can accurately reproduce the notes of the blackbird, nightingale and woodpecker.

The neat nest is made in a hedge, tree, bush, wall or shed, of grass, straw and twigs, with an inner layer of dung, mixed with saliva, and prepared to a hard consistency. Then it is lined with moss and wood chips. Four or five eggs are laid, varying in colour from blue to green, sometimes spotted black or reddish-brown, sometimes unmarked. Two or three broods may be reared, the young being fed by both parents, the older fledglings often helping to feed the younger ones.

Other thrushes include the Hebridean song thrush, missel thrush, fieldfare, blackbird, ring-ouzel and redwing.

The fieldfare

(Turdus pilaris L.)

This member of the thrush family is a winter visitor to Britain, arriving in late September and remaining until April or May. Its name means 'fieldgoer', and other popular names include *Felfer, Grey Thrush* and *Blue Back*. It is about the size of the missel thrush, and may be distinguished from other thrushes by the slate-grey colouring of its head, nape and rump. The head is streaked with black, the rump tinted buff. The back, mantle, wings and tail are dark brown, the throat and breast rich brown, streaked with black, the flanks also streaked dark brown. The belly, under wing coverts and axillaries are white. The bill is dark brown, yellow on the under mandible, and the legs are also brown.

The fieldfare is an exceptionally gregarious bird and is frequently seen on hillsides, in fields and in other open places in company with other thrushes. It is nomadic by nature and its wanderings are conditioned and regulated by the local availability of food. This consists of grubs, worms and insects, turnips and other roots, and berries. As long as the food supply is sufficient the fieldfare will remain in one place, systematically searching, ever alert to danger and invariably massing in a flock. If alarmed, the entire flock will take off down wind with angry squawks of alarm. They will then perch on nearby trees, heads facing wind. If a long flight is contemplated the flock will soar up to a considerable height, but normal flight, though powerful, is slower than that of other thrushes.

In times of severe frost, when insects are no longer available and berries likewise unobtainable, the fieldfare moves southwards, but so exceptionally sensitive is it to cold weather that it often dies of starvation or exhaustion. There are no substantiated reports of the fieldfare nesting in Britain, but both the location and construction of the nest are similar to the blackbird's; the eggs are also like those of the blackbird, though generally a deeper blue, and more thickly marked.

The missel thrush

(Turdus viscivorus L.)*

The missel, or mistle thrush derives its name from a contraction of 'mistletoe', since it was popularly believed that it fed its young entirely on the berries of this plant. In fact, this thrush, larger than the song thrush, with fewer but larger spots on its breast and greyer upper parts, enjoys a much more varied diet, including insects, snails, berries and soft fruit. It has a challenging, almost bullying nature, and has been known to kill small birds for its young.

The bird can also be distinguished from the song thrush by its flight, which is powerful, with fast wing beats alternating with prolonged periods when the wings are closed, and often at great heights. Its song is also very individual, louder and more monotonous than that of its more renowned relative, and generally delivered from high in a tree. Though not exceptionally melodious, the song takes on a wild quality at times, and when alarmed, becomes a harsh, scolding scream. Small wonder that it is often known by the names of *Screech Thrush* and *Rattle Thrush.*

Nevertheless, this indefatigable bird will resort to song at all times of year, including deep winter, and in all weathers, no matter how unpleasant. This habit of singing in torrential rain and high wind has earned it the nickname of *Storm Cock.*

The missel thrush generally nests high in forks of trees or occasionally in bushes. The nest is large, made of twigs, grass, roots and moss, and lined with mud and fine grass. Four or five eggs are laid, greenish-blue to bluish-white, and spotted brown and lilac. Two broods are raised, and the parent birds are quite fearless in protecting their nest against marauders, whether crows, hawks, cats or humans.

Almost as large as the missel thrush is the fieldfare, a spring and winter visitor to Britain. Its song is relatively feeble, however, and its flight slower. It suffers acutely from severe cold, like the redwing, and its casualties are numerous when its normal supplies of berries are exhausted, and insects no longer obtainable.

The blackbird

(Turdus merula L.)

The blackbird is an easily recognisable bird, both by sight and by ear. The male is glossy black all over, save for the orange bill and yellow eye-rim, the female dark and light brown, with dark spots on the breast. The young birds are lighter and the males do not acquire the orange beak until their second year. Some instances occur, though rarely, of pied and white birds.

It is a little larger than the song thrush, much noisier, but holding its own from the musical point of view. When alarmed, it will fly off with a shrill, complaining scream, but its normal song is most beautiful. The notes are deeper, but not as measured, nor as varied and repetitive as those of the song thrush; but the rich, flute-like whistle, sometimes heard after dark, and often as early as February, is a familiar and welcome sound in woods and gardens.

The blackbird unfortunately reaps a great deal of havoc in the garden. It eats insects and berries, raking over piles of dead leaves for them, but is inordinately fond of ripe fruit, particularly cherries and strawberries. In this respect it is far more destructive than other thrushes, and not everyone might be as patient and restrained as the essayist Addison, who wrote, 'I value my garden more for being full of blackbirds than of cherries, and very frankly give them fruit for their songs.' Most of the references to the blackbird in song, verse and nursery-rhyme are equally friendly, although the bird is not essentially a very sociable or trusting individual.

The nest is built in bushes, hedges, trees and evergreens, and is similar to those of other thrushes, being constructed of twigs, grass, straws and moss. One difference, however, is that the inner layer of mud is superimposed by an innermost lining of dried grass. It lays four or five eggs, two or three times during the season. They are bluish-green, with brown or grey spots, and sometimes unmarked.

The blackbird is a resident in Britain, but some migrate southwards, when they will congregate in large flocks. In all other respects, however, it is a strongly individual and independent bird.

The ring ouzel

(Turdus torquatus L.)

The ring ouzel is a relative of the blackbird and is in some areas known as the *Mountain Blackbird*. It spends the spring and summer in Britain after wintering in southern Europe and northern Africa, and is one of the earliest spring migrants. The ring ouzel is a bird of the mountains, moors and fells, particularly abundant in the Pennines, the Lake District, the Welsh mountains and the Scottish Highlands. In the Peak District it is called the *Tor Ouzel*. In the autumn it may descend to lower-lying areas, visiting gardens in search of ripe fruit. In other respects its diet consists of moorland berries, insects, worms and caterpillars.

In appearance the ring ouzel resembles the blackbird, but has a distinctive white crescent on its breast. Its upper parts are sooty-black, the wing feathers being bordered with grey; the under parts are also brownish-black, the under wing coverts and axillaries fringed grey and white. The female is browner and the breast band narrower and duller. The young have a mottled greyish-brown plumage.

The ring ouzel is a relatively silent bird and, as its haunts might suggest, it loves solitude. It has a clear piping call note, and its song is somewhat like that of the missel thrush, but even wilder. The quality of the song varies, however, with individual birds. The ring ouzel's flight is fast and powerful, and it has the blackbird's habit of raising and spreading the tail when alighting.

The nest may be built in a variety of places—in heather or tall grass, on a cliff ledge or hollow of a stone wall, in a derelict building, or on the ground near a stream. At times it is well concealed, at others completely exposed. It is built of bracken, moss or heather, lined with mud and grass, but unlike the blackbird's in that the grass stems are left sticking out at an angle, and are not interwoven. Four to six eggs are laid, pale greenish-blue with reddish-brown speckles and blotches. Two broods are normally raised, and the parent birds will vigorously protect their young against intruders.

The wheatear

(Oenanthe oenanthe L.)

The wheatear is the earliest of summer visitors, the first wave of male birds arriving from Africa early in March. It is a bird of the open country, pastureland, moors, downs and seashore; although fairly widely distributed, it is not commonly seen.

The adult male wheatear has grey upper parts, a white forehead and eye stripe, and black lores and ear coverts. The rump and upper tail coverts are white, the tips of the tail feathers black. It is from the white rump that the bird derives its name—there is no connection with wheat. The under parts are cream, shading to buff on the breast and flanks; the wings are black, and the under wing coverts and axillaries grey and white. The bill and the long legs are black. The female is sandy-brown above and more buff below, with brown ear coverts, but has the same white tail and rump.

The wheatear is a restless bird, flitting from stone to stone, perching for brief intervals whilst raising and lowering the tail. Its habit of sitting on an upturned clod of earth has given it one of its many nicknames, *Clodhopper*. It has a low dipping flight and during the breeding season indulges in fantastic dances and furious fights. The song, a low and pleasant warble, may sometimes be heard when the bird is in flight; at other times it utters the repeated call note which has given rise to other names like *Stone Chat*, *Chuck* and *Chacker*.

The wheatear's nest is built in any kind of hole, either in or near the ground, such as a rabbit burrow, a pile of stones, or a crevice in a wall or rock. It is a loosely woven affair of dried grass and moss, lined with hair, rabbit's fur or feathers. Five to seven eggs are laid, pale blue, sometimes faintly spotted with dark reddish-brown marks.

A bird of the same family, often confused with it, is the Greenland wheatear, which is larger and rather more brightly coloured. The two varieties mingle freely during the spring and autumn, but the Greenland wheatear is a passage migrant.

The whinchat

(Saxicola rubetra L.)

The whinchat, related to the stonechat and the wheatear, arrives in Britain in April from southern Europe and tropical Africa, and remains until September or October. It is an inhabitant of all types of grassland—meadows and pastureland, hillsides, heaths and commons, marches and rough wasteland. It is more frequently seen in the northern part of the country, perching characteristically on a bush, a stem or a telegraph wire, restlessly fanning its tail. This familiar pose has earned the bird such names as *Grasschat* and *Furzechat*.

The adult male whinchat has a conspicuous white stripe extending from the beak over and beyond the eye region. The upper parts are pale brown with darker streaks, the cheeks and ear coverts are black. The wings are brown, with two white patches, and the tail is dark brown, with white markings on each side of the base. The under parts are ruddy-buff shading to dull white on the belly; the beak, legs and feet are black. The female is paler, with browner upper parts, and the fledgling is streaked, its breast spotted with brown, and generally redder than its parents.

The whinchat is a sturdy bird but rather more slender and less erect than the stonechat, whose general habits it shares. It flits restlessly from bush to bush, capturing insects on its short darting flights, singing as it goes. The male bird has a brief, simple warble, rather metallic and somewhat like that of the redstart. Its familiar call-note has earned it the name *Utick*. For food the whinchat takes insects, spiders and worms, and has a particular liking for moths at twilight.

The whinchat's nest is usually well concealed under a bush or in bracken, or occasionally in a hollow in a field. It is made of dried grass and moss, with thinner grass and hairs to serve as lining. Five to seven eggs are laid, greenish-blue, and often finely speckled with rusty brown at the larger end. Occasionally two broods are reared.

The redstart

(Phoenicurus phoenicurus L.)

Not unlike the robin in habits, though not as strong nor as assertive, the redstart is an attractive summer guest to Britain, where it lives in woods, parkland, open hilly country, rocky ground, gardens and orchards. The name derives from an Anglo-Saxon word 'steort', meaning 'tail', and this is the bird's distinguishing feature. It is flicked constantly up and down, and from side to side, in a fashion quite unlike any other bird.

The adult male redstart has a black face and throat, white forehead and belly, rust-red rump and tail, grey crown and upper parts, orange-brown under parts, and brown wings with pale margins. The female is not as brightly garbed, but also has the distinctive red tail. The young have chestnut tails and are otherwise like young robins.

The redstart is an energetic, restless bird, hopping and flitting about like a robin in its quest for insects. It is particularly adept in catching these on the wing. The young are fed on caterpillars. Its song seems to hold out great promise at the start, a gentle warble, but rapidly peters out. More remarkable and useful is its ability to guide intruders away from its nest by a form of ventriloquism.

The peculiar, quivering motion of the tail has given rise to many nicknames, such as *Brantail*, *Flirt-tail* and *Quickstart*. During courtship, the male chases the female over the hedgerows, both birds violently agitating their tails.

The nest is constructed of dry grass, moss and roots, and is lined with hair and feathers. The location is unimportant, a hole in a tree stump, a crevice in a wall or shed, a nesting box, or an unused swallow's nest. The five or six eggs are pale blue and unmarked, a little paler and glossier than the robin's.

Not quite such a common summer visitor is the black redstart. The male has black cheeks, throat and breast, brown rump and tail, and brown wings with a white patch. It is more local in its habits and mainly seen on the south and east coasts. On the Continent, it is a familiar garden bird.

The nightingale

(Luscinia megarhyncha Brehm*)*

'Thou wast not born for death, immortal Bird!' wrote Keats in his famous *Ode to a Nightingale*. Indeed, the romantic and sentimental associations of this bird make it difficult to discuss it soberly and objectively. One charming old legend recounts how God, when painting the birds, ran out of colours before reaching the nightingale, and to compensate endowed it with a perfect voice. The contrast is very marked, as with most of the leading song birds, for the nightingale is a plain bird, similar in shape, but a little larger than the robin. Its upper parts are uniformly brown, the tail being chestnut, the under parts are greyish-brown, throat and breast nearer to white. Male and female are alike, but the young are spotted and somewhat darker.

The song of the male nightingale is its proudest possession, very difficult to describe, but unique. It is vigorous and full-throated, deep and drawn-out, a glorious medley of flute-like and rippling notes in an ascending scale, building up to a crescendo. The song is at its best shortly after sunset, and although heard in solitary splendour at night, mingles freely with that of other birds by day. Milton described the song as 'most musical, most melancholy,' and after the main song period from April until June, the characteristic note is, in fact, monotonous and plaintive.

The nightingale can be found during the summer in woods, hedgerows and gardens, and is especially attracted to well-watered districts. It has shy habits, and if venturing into the open, will keep close to cover. Its food consists of worms and insects, larvae, spiders, fruit and berries, all sought on or near the ground. Its hopping gait, with frequent flicking of wings and tail, is very reminiscent of the robin.

Its nest is generally found in undergrowth, and made of leaves and grass, with an inner lining of finer grass, roots and hairs. The four or five eggs are laid early in May, and are coloured brown or olive-green.

The robin

(Erithacus rubecula L.)

Everyone has a soft spot for 'the pious bird with the scarlet breast, Our little English robin', to quote Wordsworth's lines. Its cheeky behaviour and trusting attitude make it a universal favourite. References in poetry and nursery rhyme, not to mention Christmas cards, are innumerable.

The robin, or redbreast, is found all over the country, and is conspicuous at most times of year, especially autumn and winter. The continental variety is rather wilder in its habits, has a paler breast and is an occasional migrant to Britain.

The robin has a bright orange-red forehead, throat and breast, with a pale grey border. The upper parts are olive-brown, the lower breast and belly greyish-white. Both sexes look alike, but the young lack the orange breast and are spotted.

It is very much a bird of the undergrowth, but can be seen perching anywhere in the open, and darting across lawns in a series of lively hops. Its diet comprises insects, spiders, weed seeds, grain, berries and soft fruit, whilst in winter it will fearlessly approach houses for crumbs. Though friendly to man, it is extremely bold and pugnacious towards other birds, and indeed other robins. It appears to have a quick temper and to enjoy fighting for its own sake. Battles are fought with others of its kind over territories staked out by each bird for itself in late summer.

The robin's song is cheerful and melodious, audible throughout the year, and sometimes at night. The female also joins in the singing. If excessively angered, the robin erupts with a sharp, scolding note or hiss.

It will nest almost anywhere, in bushes or evergreen, in walls, banks or nesting boxes, even in old boots and kettles. The nest is bulky, of dry grass, leaves and moss, lined with hair, and is always cleverly hidden. Five or six eggs are laid, light blue or white, with fine reddish speckles.

The hedge sparrow

(Prunella modularis L.*)*

The plump hedge sparrow or dunnock is no relation to the house sparrow. It is really a warbler, and an unobtrusive, self-effacing bird. Its predominant colours are slate-grey and brown, the under parts being darkly streaked.

The dunnock's high-pitched warbling note, though subdued, is pleasant, and can be heard throughout the year. It perches, feeds and nests near the ground and can commonly be seen raking over leaves for insects and seeds. It progresses in a series of slow, jerky hops, or in a creeping walk, body held low and legs bent, never running.

Its nest is cleverly made and carefully concealed in a hedge, bank, bush or heap of sticks. It is made of small twigs and grass, lined with moss, hair, wool and feathers. The four to six eggs are a beautiful deep blue, unmarked.

The wren

(Troglodytes troglodytes L.*)*

The diminutive wren, though sometimes referred to ungraciously as *Stumpy Dick* and such names, has from earliest times been held sacred, and supposed to be a bringer of good fortune.

It is a short, plump bird with a tiny, upturned tail, reddish-brown above, paler beneath, barred dark brown all over, with a light stripe over the eye. It is an active, though secretive bird, always on the move, and curiously mouse-like as it scuttles about in the hedges and bushes, or along the base of a wall. The song of the male is heard all year round, a vigorous, clear and brilliant melody, remarkably loud for a bird of its size.

The nest, built in any cavity in a hedge, tree, bush, wall or thatch, or in that of a larger bird, is subtly camouflaged, dome-shaped and feather-lined, with a tiny side entrance. There are five or more eggs, white, speckled red, and there may be two or three broods.

The dipper

(Cinclus cinclus L.)*

The dipper, water-crow or water-ouzel, as it is variously called, is the only British songbird which has adapted itself to life under water. Its haunts are mainly confined to fast-flowing hill streams, but in severe weather it is known to venture into lowlands, especially near lakes and river estuaries. It resembles a large, stoutish wren both in shape and colour. Its upper parts are slate-grey mottled with black, giving an almost wholly black effect; the head is dark brown, merging into dark grey, the wings and the tail are brown. The throat and breast are white, blending into chestnut on the belly and black on the flanks. The bill is blackish, the long legs brown. Both sexes are similar, but the young have greyish-brown upper parts and lack the chestnut colouring beneath.

The dipper is a powerful flier, moving rapidly and directly to its target. The bird is more commonly seen, however, running along the banks of a stream, or perched on a rock with upraised tail. The bird's name is derived, not from its diving habits, but from its little dipping or curtseying motion when at rest. From its perch it will either walk or plunge into the swirling water in search of its diet of aquatic insects and water snails. Under the water it uses both feet and wings to propel itself, literally flying under the surface, but there is no truth in the rumour that it is able to walk along the stream bed.

The dipper's song is a melodious though brief, trilling warble, heard most frequently during the first half of the year. During courtship, the cock sings energetically whilst displaying his white plumage to his mate. More usual is the softly repeated call note.

The dipper's nest may be built in a hole in a wall, on a rock ledge, among evergreen, under a bridge or even in a dry hollow under a waterfall. The nest is a bulky domed construction of grass and moss, lined with leaves; there is a small entrance low down on one side, and the structure resembles a larger version of the wren's nest. Four to six eggs are common, pure white, and two or three broods are reared.

The swallow

(Hirundo rustica L.*)*

Popularly regarded as the herald of summer, the graceful swallow has been celebrated in poetry for many centuries. It has a slender body, long wings and a deeply forked tail, the outer feathers of the male forming long streamers. The swallow arrives in Britain in late March or early April, after a journey which may take it ten to twelve thousand miles, and leaves again in September and October for another long southward flight.

The swallow has a chestnut-red throat and forehead, glossy, metallic blue-black upper parts, a similarly coloured band encircling the throat, buff to white under parts, the tail being metallic green with white spots. The female is duller, with shorter tail streamers. Its legs are unusually short and weak, which suit it not at all for life on the ground, and it can progress only in a clumsy shuffle.

The air is the swallow's true element, and its easy graceful flight can take it up to heights of ten thousand feet or more. The wing movements are free and leisurely, and it will change direction, up and down and sideways, without any apparent break in rhythm or loss of speed. It will often glide low over a pond, sipping the water and picking insects off the surface. Other insects are captured in flight, and this method of obtaining food is common to the whole swallow tribe.

Swallows are gregarious birds, and flocks of hundreds can sometimes be seen roosting in reed beds and gathering in the sky for their winter migrations. Villages and farms are among their favourite haunts, and nests are built in rafters or on beams in sheds and out-houses, or in chimney stacks. The nest is a saucer-shaped construction of mud mixed with saliva, open at the top, and lined with grass and feathers. The four to six eggs are white, variably spotted reddish-brown or grey.

Two or three broods are raised, and the latest arrivals may get left behind in the autumn. Swallows are life mates, returning to the same village, or even to the same nesting place year after year.

The house martin

(Delichon urbica L.)

The house martin arrives in Britain from the south shortly after the swallow, and keeps even closer to houses and dwellings than its more celebrated relative. It can be distinguished by its shorter, less obviously forked tail, the white down on its legs, and the pure white under parts from chin to tail. The back and wings are a metallic blue-black. Both sexes are alike in appearance, but the young have black upper parts, and are a duller white beneath.

The house martin is not as rapid in flight as the swallow, nor does it indulge as freely in aerial acrobatics. It can, however, soar to greater heights than the swallow, and is more frequently seen perching on roof-tops and telegraph wires. It is also rather less clumsy on the ground, though it descends only to collect mud for its nest. It feeds on insects caught on the wing, mainly over water, and habitually flocks and nests in colonies. At migration time, towards autumn, swallows and martins mingle freely in preparation for their long journey.

The house martin's nesting habits are even more interesting and accomplished than those of the swallow. The nest is generally placed under the eaves of a building, and liberally plastered with mud to the wall. Both birds share in its construction, and before the work actually commences may indulge in flights of courtship and twittering conversations with each other. When completed, the nest is so strong and compact that it may be used year after year, only the lining of straw and feathers needing annual renewal. It is cup-shaped, with a tiny entrance, admitting only the parent birds. Even the house sparrow generally fails in its attempts to break into this cosy structure. It is not infrequent for a number of nests to be built adjoining one another, for like the related sand martin, it is a particularly sociable bird. The nests are almost invariably fixed to the outside walls of the building, although very occasionally they are found inside, like the swallow's.

The eggs are four or five in number, pure white, and rarely marked with red spots; as with the swallow, two or three broods are reared.

The sand martin

(Riparia riparia L.)

The third of the swallow family and the earliest to arrive from winter quarters in Africa is the sand martin. It reaches Britain shortly before the swallow, at the end of March, remaining until August or September. It is the smallest of the three varieties, just under five inches long. Its upper parts are mouse-brown, its under parts white, with a narrow brown band extending across the breast. The beak is black, the legs and feet dark brown; the wings are almost as long as the entire body, the tail is short and only slightly forked. In certain lights, the back and head appear to be almost black.

In general habits it resembles both the house martin and the swallow, but it has even more gregarious instincts than the former and is not nearly so often seen close to human habitations. Its flight is swift and graceful, and capable of attaining very considerable heights. Towards the autumn, in particular, flocks of sand martins engage in the most elaborate and complicated aerial displays, swerving and wheeling at a great height, forming long lines, and swooping down in wide spirals. At other times the birds may spend the whole day skimming from end to end of a pond or lake, twittering playfully to one another, engaging in short chases and catching insects in flight.

The sand martin is a familiar visitor in most parts of the British Isles, and especially in those places where it makes its nest—river banks, sand dunes, gravel pits, cliff faces, railway cuttings and similar natural or artificial sites. The birds nest in colonies, tunnelling horizontal passages, undisturbed if the excavations converge; the tunnels open into larger chambers, where the eggs are deposited on a simple foundation of grass, straw and feathers. They are four or five in number, white and pear-shaped, two broods being normal. At times the house sparrow puts in an unwelcome appearance, occupying a hole in the centre of a colony.

INDEX

Printed in Czechoslovakia